Atlanta Braves:
An Interactive Guide to the World of Sports

TUCKER ELLIOT

This title is part of the Sports by the Numbers series, which is a trademark owned by Daniel J. Brush, Marc CB Maxwell, and David Horne.

Cataloging-in-Publication Data is available from the Library of Congress.

ISBN: 978-0615631127
First edition, first printing.

Cover photo courtesy of Mark Whitt.

Black Mesa Publishing, LLC
Florida
Cover design by Holly Walden Ross.
Black.Mesa.Publishing@gmail.com

www.blackmesabooks.com

Also by Tucker Elliot

Kindle Singles

11 Bombs: The True Story of the 2008 Major League Home Run Derby — Josh Hamilton, Justin Morneau, and the United States Marine Corps

Relentless: A True Story of High School Baseball, Cancer, and the Boy Who Never Quit Fighting

History & Trivia

Atlanta Braves IQ: The Ultimate Test of True Fandom

New York Yankees IQ: The Ultimate Test of True Fandom

Tampa Bay Rays IQ: The Ultimate Test of True Fandom

Cincinnati Reds IQ: The Ultimate Test of True Fandom

Major League Baseball IQ: The Ultimate Test of True Fandom

Boston Red Sox: An Interactive Guide to the World of Sports

San Francisco Giants: An Interactive Guide to the World of Sports

Atlanta Braves

Sports by the Numbers
History & Trivia

CONTENTS

In Memory of Ryan Rossano

*"Swung, line drive left field! One run is in!
Here comes Bream. Here's the throw to the
plate! He is … safe! Braves win! Braves
win! Braves win! Braves win! Braves win!"*
— *Skip Caray, NLCS Game 7,
October 14, 1992*

FOREWORD

I SPENT 17 great years in the Atlanta Braves organization. I experienced the ups and downs of a minor leaguer trying to make it to the big leagues and the thrill of winning a Division Championship in 1982. Some of those years were nothing to "write home about" but a couple of MVP years were pretty special.

I'm thankful for the positive impact that the people throughout the Braves organization have had on me and on all of the Murphy family. The Braves have a storied and interesting history and I am honored to be a small part of it.

Tucker Elliot has captured that history in a way that is both educational and fun at the same time. *Atlanta Braves: An Interactive Guide to the World of Sports* is not only for those who are Braves fans, but it is also a book for anyone who loves the game of baseball.

Certainly some of the history of the Braves I know very well. But how much fun it was to discover even more about the Atlanta Braves franchise. How lucky all of us are to benefit for the work and research of Tucker Elliot because the product is something that you will enjoy reading now, and will love to revisit in the years to come.

I hope that you have as much fun as I had with *Atlanta Braves: An Interactive Guide to the World of Sports.*

Dale Murphy
Atlanta Braves, Drafted June 1974
Two-time N.L. MVP – 1982, 1983

INTRODUCTION

I GREW UP in the South and the Braves were my home team long before my parents relented and subscribed to the local cable TV network so we could watch games on TBS. My brothers and I had grown up listening to the Braves on the radio but our TV experience with baseball was limited to the nationally televised Saturday Game of the Week and Monday Night Baseball. We watched those games using the rabbit ears on our parents small black and white TV.

That changed when our neighbors got cable TV.

We lived way out in the country and they were the first family we knew who actually had cable. And when we discovered TBS broadcasted the Braves games every night at 7:05 ... well, our parents figured if they wanted us to spend more time at home then they should invest in cable. Thanks to the Braves, we got cable *and* a brand new color TV.

Of course our favorite player was Dale Murphy. The first game I remember seeing Murph play in person he homered in his first at bat. At the time my brothers and I thought that was the greatest thing that would ever happen to us. It still ranks pretty high on the list.

Like many fans, baseball was obviously an important part of my childhood and an important part of my relationship with my dad and my brothers—and in my case, with my mom as well. No one else's mom could throw BP as well as mine. My parents were very careful, however, to make sure that baseball was a tool they could use to help me grow and learn valuable life lessons. They also understood the influence that watching professional ballplayers had on young kids—so even though baseball was absolutely a positive experience in our young lives, my parents set boundaries and didn't let us have free reign. It'll sound strange nowadays I'm sure, but here's an example: we could watch the Braves on TBS or listen to a game on the radio no problem, but if our parents were not in the room with us then the rule was we had to turn the volume down during commercials.

I get that it might sound like a strange rule today ... but the truth is we didn't question it because it was a boundary our parents set for us and we just accepted it. And looking back I appreciate it— because our parents knew how impressionable we were, how much we idolized the Braves and the guys who wore that uniform, and how easily influenced we were by anything associated with our favorite team. In other words, they had standards—and they wanted to make sure people and products that met those standards influenced us.

And that's why our parents were more than happy to let Dale Murphy be our baseball hero.

After all, the guy did milk ads.

In my adult life I've been a baseball coach, an athletic director, and a teacher—and I've spent a lot of time worrying about who my student-athletes idolize. Today I spend all my time writing, but when I shoot hoops and talk NBA with my nephew or go see a Rays or Braves game with my nieces I still worry about who is influencing them. And I wish the guys who were glorified during baseball's steroids era hadn't been treated like gods at the time. I wish we lived in a simpler time when parents could tell their kids to turn down the volume during commercials—but in the tech-savvy world we live in, kids today have a much different reality. And they need boundaries more than ever, and everyone knows we need athletes to be better role models—but kids today also need tools to help them make good choices in life.

All that to say this—I'm glad there are organizations like Dale Murphy's I Won't Cheat Foundation. I'm glad there are athletes with standards and morals who kids can look up to and learn from. I'm glad that for every bad example my nephew sees today on ESPN that I can share with him stories about truly heroic ballplayers like Cal Ripken, Jr. or Dale Murphy or Kirby Puckett.

The I Won't Cheat Foundation's motto is "Injecting Ethics into America's Future."

I like it, a lot—and I think every fan of baseball should support the principles that I Won't Cheat promotes. You can visit IWontCheat.com to learn more about the comprehensive program available for schools and youth leagues.

This book is about the history of the Atlanta Braves. In it you will find the greatest players and moments in franchise history. It's my hope that you will also find the same positive message in these pages that Dale Murphy's Foundation promotes—that character and integrity matter, and goals we achieve with our character and integrity intact have real value.

Tucker Elliot
Tampa, FL
March 2012

"He always protected his players."
— Randy Marsh, retired MLB umpire, in
a video tribute on "Bobby Cox Day"

1 BOBBY COX

THE ATLANTA BRAVES retired Bobby Cox's #6 jersey on August 12, 2011, during an emotional pregame ceremony on "Bobby Cox Day." That same day he was inducted into the Braves Hall of Fame, after which he said, "It's very humbling to be inducted into any Hall of Fame. I think the Braves Hall of Fame is very special. It's been a great day ... it brings back a lot of memories."

There are many ways to measure a manager's success and contributions to a franchise—and what follows is a look at the numbers that have made Bobby Cox such an integral part of Braves history—but in this case the two numbers that illustrate it best are eight and four: Bobby Cox's #6 jersey was just the eighth number retired in franchise history, and of the remaining seven ... four of them played for Bobby.

1 Bobby Cox spent parts of 1968-69 playing third base for the New York Yankees—and that was the extent of his Major League playing career. It wasn't for a lack of trying, there's no quit in this guy, as Braves fan will attest. Cox spent parts of ten seasons from 1960-71 playing various levels of Minor League ball—including four full seasons at Triple-A. So ... what's #1 for? I'm not sure Bobby was ever fleet-footed ... but on August 5, 1968, against Baltimore's Dave McNally, Bobby Cox legged out the (1st) and only *inside-the-park* home run of his career.

2 The 1990s were very good to the Atlanta Braves. It was a far cry from the mid to late-80s. With Bobby Cox at the helm, the Braves franchise was named *Baseball America* Organization of the Year (2) times during the decade: 1991 and 1996.

4 Bobby Cox will enter the Hall of Fame because of his managerial career with the Braves. He won Manager of the Year (4) times in his career: in 1985 with the Toronto Blue Jays, and 1991, 2004, and 2005 with the Atlanta Braves. If you want to have a debate on Cox's career ... I'd suggest he should have been Manager of the Year in 1993 as well.

5 Bobby Cox won (5) NL Pennants: 1991, 1992, 1995, 1996, and 1999. His Toronto Blue Jays were robbed of a Pennant in 1985, and I guess a lot of fans are disappointed that Cox *only* won five during his tenure with the Braves ... not me. I grew up a diehard Braves fan. Watching my hometown team play in the World Series five times in the 1990s ... very, very cool. Thanks, Bobby.

6 The Braves announced in March 2011 that Bobby's (#6) jersey would be retired on "Bobby Cox Day" on August 12, 2011. Just the eighth number retired by the franchise, upon hearing the news, Cox said, "I'm honored. I'm humbled. I honestly don't know if I belong up there with those numbers." Get used to it, Bobby—next stop, Cooperstown.

8 The 14-year run of Division Titles was impressive—but in that stretch, Bobby Cox also led the Braves to a MLB record (8) consecutive appearances in the NLCS from 1991-99. That streak came to an end when the Braves lost the 2000 Division Series to the St. Louis Cardinals.

9 Bobby Cox hit a total of (9) Major League home runs and they came against some pretty familiar names: Gary Peters, Denny McLain, Dave McNally, Dick Ellsworth, Dave Boswell, Jim Kaat, Pat Dobson, and Phil Ortega. He never hit two in a single game, but three of his bombs came in his home park: Yankee Stadium. He also homered on the road in Minnesota, Chicago, Boston, Washington, and Detroit. You might have noticed there are only eight names on the list of pitchers who served up a long ball to Bobby. If you did, then nice catch—it's because Bobby's first and last career home runs came against the same pitcher: Gary Peters. Bobby took him yard on May 26, 1968, for his first Major League home run ... and he took him yard on August 15, 1969, for his final Major League home run.

14 Thanks, Bobby, for (14) consecutive Division Titles—the longest such streak in Major League history: 1991, 1992, 1993, (no postseason in 1994), 1995, 1996, 1997, 1998, 1999, 2000, 2001, 2002, 2003, 2004, and 2005.

15 Under Bobby's leadership, the 2000 Atlanta Braves won a modern-era franchise record (15) consecutive games from April 16 – May 2. It was the longest winning streak in MLB since the New York Giants won 16 consecutive games in 1951.

18 And speaking of streaks ... one of the most astounding but least talked about streaks in franchise history began on May 15, 2002. Atlanta began play that day at 19-21, having lost three straight and in fourth place, 3.5 games out of first. It was only May, but there were many who were predicting the Braves run of Division Titles was doomed. Not so fast. The Bobby Cox led Braves beat the Giants 6-1, and the next day beat the Giants again, 5-4, to salvage a split of the four-game series. Atlanta then won 60 of its next 80 games and during that stretch won an extraordinary (18) out of its next 21 series—and even more remarkable, the three series that Atlanta didn't win were all splits. The Braves did not lose a single series from May 15 until July 28, when they lost the finale of a three-game set vs. the Phillies. By that point, however, the club was in first place with a 12.5 game lead ... and on September 9, the Braves clinched yet another Division Title, this time by 19 games and on the earliest date in franchise history.

37 Fans know Bobby was with the Braves for a long time … but go back and look at photos from 1978. That's right. You'd be looking at a (37)-year-old first-year manager. Bobby was 69 when he left the club in 2010.

81 Atlanta was 19-11 and 15-11 during August and September 1980 … and at one point during that stretch the club reached a season high eight games above .500. After losing three of four to end September, however, and then losing four of five in October, the Braves closed out the season with (81) wins—one game above .500 after playing a 161-game schedule. The 81 wins were easily the highest total during Bobby's first tenure with the Braves.

88 The lowest wins total for any of Bobby's 14 Division-winning Braves clubs was (88) in 2001. Bobby took the Braves to the postseason 15 times—the other 14 clubs won at least 90 games and 11 of them won at least 94.

99 Bobby took over managerial duties for the Toronto Blue Jays in 1982. His teams found ways to improve every year: 78 wins, then 89, 89, and finally a league-best (99) wins in 1985 to claim the American League East Division by two games over the New York Yankees. Against the Royals in the ALCS, Cox led the Blue Jays to a 3-1 series lead … but cold bats and bad calls *(Jesse Barfield come to mind?)* let the eventual World Champion Royals rally to claim the AL Pennant.

125 Bobby's short Major League career was due to a number of factors and you can debate them as much as you'd like—but don't make the mistake of saying he couldn't hit. Cox blasted (125) bombs in the minors—including six seasons in which he hit 16 or more home runs. He hit a career high 21 in only 126 games in 1963, splitting time between Great Falls and Albuquerque.

158 No accounting of Bobby's career would be complete without mentioning the (158) times he was ejected from a regular season ballgame. Bobby surpassed the previous record 131 ejections held by Hall of Famer John McGraw on August 14, 2007, when home plate umpire Ted Barrett tossed him for arguing a called third strike against Chipper Jones. Ironically, the ejection came against the Giants, the franchise McGraw managed for 31 years. Cox said of his record, "It means nothing. It just means I've been around for a long time. That's all." Chipper Jones took a different viewpoint, saying, "I'm kind of glad that the record came on behalf of me. To be honest with you, Bobby has been kind of biting his tongue lately because he's embarrassed by the record. But it was inevitable. He just gets too excited and is passionate about the game." Bobby was also ejected three times in the postseason—twice in the World Series (1992 and 1996) and during Game 2 of the 2010 Division Series vs. San Francisco.

412 Bobby replaced Russ Nixon for his second tour of duty as manager with 97 games left on the 1990 schedule. The club was 40-57 the rest of the way, for a (.412) winning percentage that left the Braves dead last in the league with an overall 65-97 record.

557 The winning percentage (.557) for Bobby Cox after managing a franchise record 25 seasons and 3,860 regular season games. His won-loss totals are obviously both franchise records as well: 2,149 wins, 1,709 losses.

580 Let's say it all together now: "WORST-TO-FIRST!" It never gets old. Dead last in 1990, just one year later Bobby led the 1991 Atlanta Braves to a 94-68 record, good for a (.580) winning percentage. Atlanta trailed LA by one game on October 1, but the Dodgers lost three straight, and the Braves won three straight ... and clinched the NL West on October 5, 1991.

616 The Braves surpassed the century mark in wins six times during Bobby's tenure: 1993, 1997, 1998, 1999, 2002, and 2003. Atlanta won (616) games during those six seasons. Perhaps the most impressive stretch was 1997-99, when the Braves were 310-176, easily the best three-year run in franchise history. When the Braves hit the century mark in 2002, Bobby Cox became the first National League manager to claim five 100-win seasons, which means ... in 2003 he was, obviously, the first to claim six 100-win seasons.

625 Bobby led Atlanta to an impressive (.625) winning percentage during the 1995 World Championship season. The Braves won 90 games despite the abbreviated 144-game schedule due to the work stoppage that cancelled the 1994 postseason and threatened the 1995 season as well. To put those 90 wins into perspective ... the rest of the NL East: New York Mets (69 wins), Philadelphia Phillies (69 wins), Florida Marlins (67 wins), and the Montreal Expos (66 wins). The Braves won the Division by 21 games—but only *three games* separated the teams that finished 2nd through last in the Division. Cincinnati won the Central Division with 85 victories and LA won the West with just 78 wins.

654 Bobby's best winning percentage was (.654) when the 1998 Atlanta Braves posted a ridiculous 106-56 record during the regular season. The Braves finished 18 games in front of the second place New York Mets and an astounding 52 games in front of the last place Florida Marlins—just one season after the Wild Card Marlins had won the World Series. After sweeping the Cubs in the 1998 Division Series, the heavily favored Braves were unfortunately upset by the San Diego Padres during a six-game NLCS.

750 The Braves posted a 21-7 record that included a season-best ten-game winning streak during August 1999—good for a (.750) winning percentage for the month. With the club's Division Title streak being threatened by a very good Mets team (the clubs were tied for first as late as August 21), Bobby led the Braves to a torrid finish that included a 19-9 record in September and October. All total the Braves closed out the season by winning 40 of their final 56 games to put away the hated Mets and wrap up another NL East Title by 6.5 games. The Mets won the Wild Card, however—and the two clubs met again in the NLCS. The Braves won a hard-fought series in six games for the final NL Pennant of Bobby Cox's career.

1,632 Atlanta spent (1,632) days in first place during its run of 14-consecutive Division Titles. The fewest came in 1991 when the unprecedented streak began with just 27 days spent on top of the standings. The most impressive stretch was from 1997-2000, when the Braves spent at least 163 days in first place during four consecutive seasons—including 175 days in 2000, the highest total during Bobby Cox's 14 seasons leading the Braves to Division Titles.

52,613 The number of fans (52,613) in attendance for the 2010 season finale at Turner Field vs. the Philadelphia Phillies. In Bobby Cox's last regular season game as manager the Braves needed a win and a Padres loss to clinch the National League Wild Card. Tim Hudson took the mound and the offense took a six-run lead, but in the end the Braves had to hold on for a nail biting 8-7 victory. The Giants beat the Padres later in the day, and in his final season Bobby Cox once again led the Atlanta Braves into the postseason. "We try hard. This team is the hardest-working, hardest-trying team we've ever had here," Cox said afterwards.

"I think it's a mistake to see it as an overnight phenomenon. These guys drafted very well. Steve Avery didn't show up in Atlanta by mistake."
— *Fay Vincent, Baseball Commissioner, on the Braves success in 1991*

2 WORST TO FIRST

THE ATLANTA BRAVES signed three key free agents in December 1990—Terry Pendleton (St. Louis) and Sid Bream (Pittsburgh) were signed away from teams in the NL East, and Charlie Leibrandt inked a new deal with the Braves after posting a 9-11 record in his first season with the last place Braves. Atlanta made another key acquisition in April 1991 as the new season was getting underway, trading two players to Montreal in exchange for Otis Nixon.

There were no A-Rod-esque deals ... and there were no big names like Fielder or Pujols dominating the free agent market. In fact, America's Team had drawn the ire of fans everywhere by trading Dale Murphy to the Philadelphia Phillies in August 1990—so in terms of news stories, the transactions that followed didn't generate much interest.

Not for a while, anyway.

Ten months later the Braves were NL Champions, Bobby Cox was the NL Manager of the Year, John Schuerholz was the NL Executive of the Year, and the Atlanta Braves were named Organization of the Year by *Baseball America*. Here are the numbers that tell the story of how the Braves went from "worst to first."

1 Atlanta became the (1st) team in league history to win the NL Pennant after finishing the previous season with the worst record in baseball. The 1990 Braves were dead last in league attendance as well, with just over 980,000 fans taking in games at Fulton County Stadium. On the field, the pitching staff gave up the most runs and the second most walks in the league. The 1990 club won just 65 games and finished 26 games back of Cincinnati in the NL West. The 1991 club, however, was a different story …

40 Bobby Cox replaced Russ Nixon after Nixon lost (40) of 65 games he managed in 1990. Cox, however, won just (40) of the 97 games he managed that season. Perhaps no number shows how dramatic the turnaround was between 1990 and 1991, as does …

55 Bobby Cox led the Braves to (55) wins *in the second half* of the 1991 season. Atlanta was 55-28 after the 1991 All-Star break. Good thing, too—as the Braves entered the break trailing the first place Dodgers by 9.5 games. Atlanta caught fire, starting the season's second half 9-2, and just like that the Braves had trimmed the deficit to only 2.5 games.

108 Atlanta played its (108th) game on August 10 with John Smoltz, Mike Stanton, and Juan Berenguer combining on a 4-0, four-hit shutout vs. Houston. Two weeks earlier the Braves had fallen to six games back in the standings, but with the shutout vs. the Astros, the Braves were back to only 2.5 games behind the Dodgers. Atlanta swept the series vs. Houston the next day, surrendering only three runs total in the three-game series, and for the rest of the season the Braves and Dodgers were in an intense dogfight for the Division Title, with the distance between the two clubs never being more than 2.5 games.

139 The Braves took the field on September 11 for the (139th) game of the regular season after having won five straight to take a .5 game lead over the Dodgers. It was a magical night: Kent Mercker earned his fifth win of the season with six scoreless innings, Mark Wohlers came on in relief and retired all six batters he faced in two innings of work, and Alejandro Pena closed it out in the ninth, preserving a 1-0 victory. And oh yeah … those three combined for a no-hitter. It was the first combined no-no in franchise history, and the first overall for the club since Phil Niekro in 1973, but it wasn't without controversy: with two outs in the ninth, Darrin Jackson hit a high chopper to third baseman Terry Pendleton who moved to his left before inexplicably pulling away his glove, allowing the ball to get past him where a surprised Rafael Belliard, the Braves shortstop, kicked it, allowing Jackson to reach first. It was ruled an error by official scorer Mark Frederickson, despite the fact Pendleton later said he lost the ball in the lights. True, some media associated with the Padres thought it should have been ruled a hit, but Braves broadcaster Pete Van Wieren said, "When that happens, I put myself on the other side. If that was the Braves being no-hit and that was an error, would I have been upset? I wouldn't have been."

158 The drama was just beginning for the 1991 Braves—on October 1, playing their (158th) game of the regular season and trailing the Dodgers by a single game in the standings, Atlanta fell behind Cincinnati 6-0 in the first inning. Charlie Leibrandt started and got shelled for the Braves, giving up a walk, double, double, walk, single, walk, and home run to successive batters. It would have been 7-0 except right fielder David Justice gunned down Chris Sabo trying to stretch a double into a triple. Enter Pete Smith, Mike Bielecki, Mike Stanton, and Alejandro Pena, who combined to pitch six scoreless innings of three-hit relief. The Braves scored twice in the fourth, a run in the fifth, two more in the seventh, and then trailing 6-5 in the ninth … David Justice, again. This time at the plate, he launched a two-run game-winning home run against ace closer Rob Dibble. The Dodgers also won that night, but Justice's heroics kept the Braves only one game back, with four to play.

159 Atlanta took the field on October 2 for the (159th) time. It was also the Braves sixth straight—and final—road game of the regular season, and they were playing with a tired bullpen. Atlanta began its final road trip of the season trailing the Dodgers by two games, but after winning the first five games on the trip, Tom Glavine took the mound in Cincinnati and he was literally a man on a mission. Perhaps no one player illustrated better the Braves drastic change in fortune from one year to the next—only three years earlier, Glavine had led the league with 17 losses and he'd been just 10-12 in 1990. As he toed the rubber on October 2, 1991, however, he was seeking to pitch his team into a tie atop the NL West standings ... and at the same time, to become the Majors first 20-game winner of the season. He did both, as this time it was the Braves who scored six runs in the first—only Glavine, unlike the Reds staff the night before, refused to budge at all. He tossed eight innings and gave up just one earned run as the Braves won 6-3. With the Dodgers losing that night, Glavine and the Braves were now tied for the Division lead ... with three games left. Asked about his remarkable achievement, Glavine said, "It's a big accomplishment but I think it will mean more to me during the winter because there are some other things going on now."

160 Prior to the Braves 6-0 road trip, Bobby Cox was asked if it was possible to gain ground on the Dodgers while playing six games on the road in the season's final days (the Dodgers, meanwhile, had six straight at home vs. San Francisco and San Diego). Cox answered, "I don't know that we need to win every game. I do know that we sure can't afford to lose too many more." After winning six straight, Cox said with a wry grin, "A 5-1 trip would have been a disaster." Atlanta's final series was at home vs. last place Houston. The series opener was the Braves (160th) game of the season and this time it was Steve Avery's turn to shine—he improved to 18-8 on the season with eight innings of three-hit ball, and the Braves won 5-2. The Dodgers lost 4-1 in San Francisco, and with two games left on the schedule the Braves were alone in first by a single game.

161 The *Atlanta Journal and Constitution* called it the "Miracle on Capital Avenue" when the Braves beat the Astros again, 5-2, on October 5, in the (161st) game of the regular season—and then along with 45,000 screaming fans the players turned to the jumbo TV screen at Atlanta's Fulton County Stadium to witness the final out of the Giants 4-0 victory over the Dodgers, and just like that, the Braves had gone from "worst-to-first." Greg Olson, the Braves catcher, said, "I thought, I'm going to break down and cry and the game isn't even over. But I held back, and then that final out. It's so emotional, so emotional."

162 After (162) games the NL West Division champs closed out the season with a record of 94-68. The 94 wins set a record at the time for the Atlanta era of franchise history—as for attendance, well, the resilient 1991 club drew a then-record 2,140,217 fans, a far cry from the dismal 1990 season. Some numbers regarding the regular season schedule: Atlanta spent just 27 days in first, compared to 135 for the Dodgers; Atlanta's eight-game winning streak that clinched the Division was its longest of the season; the Braves never led the Division by more than two games, while the Dodgers held a six-game lead over all teams on July 28, and a 9.5 game lead over the Braves as late as July 7; but the biggest difference, Atlanta was 55-28 after the break, while the Dodgers were just 44-38.

255 Tom Glavine was third in the league with a (2.55) earned run average—but he was tied for first in the league with 20 wins, second in the league with 246-plus innings pitched, third in the league with a walks plus hits per nine innings ratio (WHIP) of just 1.095, fifth in the league with 7.005 strikeouts per nine innings, and ... you get the idea: Glavine was the overwhelming choice for NL Cy Young honors, taking home 19 of the possible 24 first place votes. Glavine became the first pitcher in the Atlanta era of franchise history to win the award, and he was the first lefty to win 20 games for the Braves since Warren Spahn in 1963. After winning his 20th game of the season, Glavine gave pitching coach Leo Mazzone a bottle of champagne with a card that said, "When you pop this, think of me." After Glavine won the Cy Young Award, however, Mazzone said, "I'm looking at that bottle right now, but I'll promise you, it will never be opened."

274 Terry Pendleton signed with the Braves as a free agent after 1990, and his acquisition was an integral part of the Braves "worst-to-first" 1991 Pennant-winning season. Pendleton made an immediate impact, batting .324 with eight home runs and 34 RBIs during the first half of the season—but he did even better in the second half when the Braves surged and caught the Dodgers in the race for the Division Title. He batted .315 with 14 home runs and 52 RBIs after the All-Star break, and for his efforts he received (274) points in MVP balloting, edging out Barry Bonds—who garnished 259 points—to win NL MVP honors. When told he'd won the award, Pendleton said, "This is something I never figured would be within my grasp." The man who brought him to Atlanta, General Manager John Schuerholz, said, "It's hard to separate what Terry meant on the field and off the field. The package was so important. It's a great honor for the whole organization."

319 Pendleton's (.319) batting average was also tops in the league, giving him a batting title and MVP honors. Asked what such an extraordinary accomplishment meant to him personally, Pendleton said, "What I really wanted this year was a World Championship ring."

377 Outfielders Lonnie Smith and David Justice each posted a (.377) on-base percentage—nowhere near the league leader board, but still the best on the club. Smith was a veteran leader with serious playoff experience and three rings to prove it, and Justice was a sophomore slugger who was too fearless to know or care that the Braves weren't supposed to be contenders. Roaming the corners of the outfield, each would leave his mark on the Braves miraculous run of postseasons that began in 1991.

496 Ron Gant led the club with 32 home runs, 105 RBIs, and 101 runs scored—but his (.496) slugging percentage was only third best behind Terry Pendleton, .517, and David Justice, .503. The Braves centerfielder added another dimension to the Braves offense, however: *speed.* Gant stole 34 bases, which made him a member of the prestigious 30/30 club. Gant was the third player in franchise history to join the 30/30 ranks behind Hank Aaron (1963) and Dale Murphy (1983), however … Gant actually did one better than Aaron and Murphy. That's because he was a member of the 30/30 club in 1990 as well—which made Gant the first player in franchise history to post *back-to-back* 30/30 seasons.

1991 League Championship Series

7 The 1991 NLCS was one of the most exciting (7)-game series in league history. Atlanta took the field at Three Rivers Stadium on Wednesday, October 9, for Game 1—the first postseason game for the Braves since 1982—and faced a Pirates team that was statistically the best in baseball. With 98 wins the Pirates won the NL East by 14 games over the second place Cardinals—and the Pirates offense, paced by Barry Bonds, Andy Van Slyke, and Bobby Bonilla, was the highest scoring in the league. Pittsburgh's pitching staff was no joke either—led by John Smiley (20-8), Zane Smith (16-10), and Doug Drabek (15-14), the Pirates were second only to the Dodgers in team earned run average (the Braves staff was a close third). Just how good was the pitching in this series? Four of the seven games were shutouts, and Games 2, 5, and 6 were all decided by the same score: 1-0.

60 The Pirates outfield trio of Bonds, Van Slyke, and Bonilla combined for (60) home runs in the regular season. And it didn't take long for them to get on the board in the postseason, either. In his first career postseason start, Tom Glavine retired Gary Redus and Jay Bell on a fly ball and a strikeout to start the home half of the first, but he made a mistake on a 3-2 pitch to Van Slyke, batting third, who ripped a line drive to deep right field for a 1-0 Pirates lead. Atlanta's 20-game winner gave up just six hits in six innings of work, but he also gave up four earned runs—and the Braves lost the opener 5-1. Van Slyke had two hits and two RBIs in the game, however ...

148 Barry Bonds batted just (.148) for the series and the Game 1 home run by Van Slyke was the only bomb in the series for the Pirates vaunted outfielders. As a team the Pirates hit just three home runs and batted just .224—Bonds had no RBIs and scored just one run, Bonilla scored twice and had one RBI, and Van Slyke had only two additional hits and no RBIs after his big Game 1 performance.

234 Steve Avery threw (234) pitches during the NLCS—and in 16-plus innings of work he didn't allow a single run. To say the 21-year-old lefty stepped up his game is an understatement of epic proportions. Yes, he'd won 18 games in the regular season, but what he did during the NLCS was just ridiculous. Avery made 118 pitches during eight-and-a-third shutout innings in Game 2. Atlanta held on for a 1-0 victory, with David Justice scoring the game's only run on a two-out, sixth inning double by Mark Lemke. Atlanta's offense showed up in Game 3 and the Braves won easily, 10-3. It was a different story in Games 4 and 5—both games were decided by a single run, and the Pirates won them both. And then it was Avery's turn again … Game 6, on the road, facing elimination … and all he did was throw 116 pitches in eight shutout innings. The Braves offense managed to score two runs *total* in Avery's two starts … yet won both games, 1-0.

257 The Pirates pitching staff posted an impressive (2.57) earned run average for the series. Thanks in large part to Avery, the Series MVP, Atlanta's pitching staff was not only better, they were an *entire run* better, posting a 1.57 earned run average. In fact, Pittsburgh scored only one run in the final 27 innings of the series—and didn't score at all after the fifth inning of Game 5. The Braves offense struck early in Game 7—Ron Gant hit a sacrifice fly in the top of the first for a 1-0 lead, and two batters later Brian Hunter blasted a two-run shot to make it 3-0. Then John Smoltz took the mound and it was lights out, game over—a complete game 4-0 shutout, 123 pitches, six hits and only one walk, and eight strikeouts. Smoltz took the mound in the ninth and retired the side in order, completing the "worst to first" turnaround and giving Atlanta its first Pennant since the franchise moved from Milwaukee.

1991 World Series

74 After winning just (74) games in 1990 and placing dead last in the AL West, the Minnesota Twins incredibly won 95 games for the best record in the AL in 1991. The Twins won the ALCS vs. Toronto in five games, setting up a true "worst-to-first" showdown with the

Braves in the World Series. It was the first time in history that two teams contested the Fall Classic after both finished last respectively in the previous season. Minnesota's turnaround was fueled by an offense that led the league in average and was fourth in runs, a pitching staff that was the second stingiest in the AL, and a defensive unit that had the second highest fielding percentage in the league. Add in the charismatic leadership of Kirby Puckett, the fact the Twins held home field advantage based on the odd-numbered year awarding that privilege automatically to the AL Champion, that the Metrodome was a loud, almost impossible atmosphere for a visiting club, especially one from the NL, and that the Twins held the best home record in the AL that season … and it's clear how difficult a challenge the Braves were up against.

234 Mark Lemke batted (.234) during the regular season but the switch-hitting infielder is the perfect example to illustrate how little the Braves cared about the noise in the Metrodome, the Twins record at home, or having to start the series on the road. Atlanta's Pennant-winning campaign was every bit as surprising as was the Twins, unless you were in uniform, of course. Lemmer and the rest of the team took the field every night believing they belonged on baseball's biggest stage—hence, the .234 hitter in the regular season batted .417 in the World Series with ten hits, four runs, a double, three triples and four RBIs. He'd hit only two triples in the regular season, and he was the first player in 44 years to hit three in a single World Series. And yet, Lemmer's play was even more impressive than those numbers illustrate. That's because after losing Games 1 and 2 in Minnesota, the Braves faced a must-win situation at home in Game 3. Tied 4-4 in the bottom of the twelfth, Lemmer hit a two-out game-winning single that plated David Justice and got the Braves back into the series. In Game 4, tied 2-2 in the ninth, Lemmer tripled with one out to set up a second consecutive walk-off win. Two batters later he scored the winning run on a Jerry Willard sacrifice fly, and the series was tied two games apiece.

270 Tom Glavine's earned run average (2.70) during the 1991 World Series. In two starts in the NLCS, Glavine had posted a 3.21 earned run average—despite that, Atlanta's 20-game winner during the regular season took the mound for Game 5 vs. the Twins with a 0-3 record during the postseason. He'd lost Games 1 and 5 of the NLCS, and he'd suffered a tough 3-2 loss in Game 2 of the World Series despite pitching a complete game and yielding only four hits. Game 5 had that same feel until the bottom of the fourth when the Braves plated four runs, and by the end of the eighth the Braves offense had plated more runs than it had in Games 1 through 4 combined. Atlanta won easily, 14-5. Glavine said afterwards, "I feel darn good to get that win and help this team. I sure didn't want to go into the offseason knowing I was 0-4 in the playoffs and World Series." Strong starts by Steve Avery and John Smoltz in Games 3 and 4 and late inning heroics by Mark Lemke had tied the series, and now Glavine and a resurgent offense had given the Braves a 3-2 advantage in the best-of-seven series. All they had to do was win one game in Minnesota ...

577 Lonnie Smith homered in three straight games in Atlanta and he posted a (.577) slugging percentage for the series. Unfortunately, a Kirby Puckett walk-off home run in Game 6 tied the series and forced a deciding Game 7 ... and in that decisive game, Lonnie Smith made a base running blunder that overshadowed everything else he'd done in the series. Smith was already a three-time World Champion and his veteran presence was invaluable, but in the eighth inning of a scoreless game he could have scored from first on a double by Terry Pendleton, only Twins second baseman Chuck Knoblauch deked him, and made him think the ball had been thrown to the infield already. Smith hesitated just enough that he had to stop at third, and he never scored ...

55,118 There were (55,118) fans at the Metrodome for Game 7, and for the seventh and final time in the series the home team left happy. They were quiet in the eighth, however, as the Braves had runners on second and third with no outs following the Pendleton double. Smith isn't entirely to blame for the Braves failing to score, as Ron Gant hit a weak grounder to first that failed to produce a run. After David Justice was intentionally walked, Sid Bream grounded into a double play to end the threat. It might be frustrating as a Braves fan, but you also have to stop and admire Jack Morris for staying out there. The Twins starter pitched *ten innings* of shutout baseball during Game 7 of the World Series. It doesn't get more impressive than that. Smoltzie was great for the Braves, pitching scoreless ball into the eighth. In that same frame, the Twins also loaded the bases with only one out but failed to score when Mark Lemke snared a line drive off the bat of Kent Hrbek and stepped on the bag at second to double up Chuck Knoblauch. In the end, however, Gene Larkin won it for the Twins in walk-off fashion. Scoreless in the tenth, Dan Gladden led off with a double. A sacrifice bunt and two intentional walks later, Larkin batted with the bases loaded and one out … and sent a deep fly to left over the drawn in outfield to give the series to the Twins. Despite the loss, the Braves still had a celebratory parade back home in Atlanta before going their separate ways for the offseason, after which Ron Gant said, "I don't think anybody is sad because they realize what we are going to have coming back next year. This is just the beginning of something that is going to be good for a long time." Not sure how much weight people gave his statement in 1991, but for sure he got that right.

"I don't know where Hank Aaron will break Ruth's record but I can tell you one thing—ten years from the day he hits it, three million people will say they were there."
— Eddie Mathews

3 THE LEGENDS

HALL OF FAME legend Hank Aaron said in his induction speech, "It was not fame I sought, but rather the best baseball player that I could possibly be." Aaron, of course, became the greatest player of his generation and one of the greatest legends in baseball history. Not every franchise can claim such a legend as its own—but the Braves have Hammerin' Hank.

There are currently eleven players enshrined as a Brave at Cooperstown: Hank Aaron (Milwaukee, 1982), John Clarkson (Boston Beaneaters, 1963), Hugh Duffy (Boston Beaneaters, 1945) Rabbit Maranville (Boston Braves, 1954), Eddie Mathews (Milwaukee, 1978), Tommy McCarthy (Boston Beaneaters, 1946), Kid Nichols (Boston Beaneaters, 1949), Phil Niekro (Atlanta, 1997), Frank Selee (Boston Beaneaters, 1999), Warren Spahn (Milwaukee, 1973), and Vic Willis (Boston Braves, 1995). In this chapter the numbers tell the stories behind three of these Hall of Fame legends—Aaron, Mathews, and Spahn—plus an Atlanta legend not in the Baseball Hall of Fame, Dale Murphy, and some modern legends who one day will be enshrined at Cooperstown.

Hank Aaron

4 Hank Aaron led the league in home runs (4) times during his 23 Major League seasons. That's only half as many times as Mike Schmidt's NL record eight home run titles, and it's only a third as many times as the Major League record 12 titles won by Babe Ruth, but for Hammerin' Hank it wasn't about leading the league—it was about consistency, and in that department no one did it better. Aaron hit 30-plus home runs a record 15 times and from 1955-73 his lowest season total was 24.

44 The jersey number (44) retired in honor of Hank Aaron. Originally he wore #5, but changed his number after a fractured ankle on September 5, 1954, ended his rookie season. The move to #44 was a good one—Aaron would hit exactly 44 home runs in a season four times during his career. He hit more than 40 home runs eight times, including a career high 47 in 1971.

50 Hank Aaron signed with the Indianapolis Clowns in 1951. The 18-year-old from Mobile, Alabama relocated to Indiana to pursue a career in professional baseball and that first season he helped the Clowns win the 1952 Negro League World Series. Aaron batted .366 that season with five homers and 33 RBIs in 26 official games. His stellar play earned him two offers from Major League teams—the Braves and the New York Giants. Aaron chose the Braves because the contract was ($50) a month more than what the Giants offered. Years later Aaron said, "I had the Giants contract in my hand but the Braves offered me fifty dollars a month more. That's the only thing that kept Willie Mays and me from being teammates—fifty dollars."

322 Aaron was only 23 when he batted (.322) in 1957—fourth best in the league. He narrowly missed winning the Triple Crown, as he led the league with 44 home runs and 132 RBIs. It was a banner year to say the least—in addition to winning league MVP honors, Aaron also had what he calls one of the greatest moments of his career on September 23 vs. St. Louis. Aaron hit a two-run walk-off home run in the eleventh inning—and it was that victory that sealed the

Pennant for the Braves. His teammates carried him from the field that day.

500 Aaron's (500th) career home run came vs. Mike McCormick of the San Francisco Giants on July 14, 1968. At the time he became just the eighth member and the second youngest to join the 500 Home Run Club. Two years later, on May 17, 1970, Aaron also joined the 3,000 Hit Club—thus becoming the first player in history to reach 3,000 hits and 500 home runs. Willie Mays, Eddie Murray, and Rafael Palmeiro later achieved that same feat.

Eddie Mathews

1 Eddie Mathews belongs to an exclusive club that has just (1) member: he is the only player in franchise history who played for the Braves in Boston, Milwaukee, and Atlanta. Mathews was a rookie during the Braves final season in Boston in 1952, he was with the club in Milwaukee from 1953-65, and his final season with the Braves was 1966—the year the franchise first played in Atlanta.

41 The jersey number (41) retired in honor of Eddie Mathews. Inducted into the Hall of Fame in 1978, Mathews is one of the greatest third basemen in Major League history. Like Hank Aaron, Mathews was a model of consistency: he hit 25 home runs as a 20-year-old rookie in 1952—including three in one game vs. Brooklyn on September 27—and then he proceeded to hit at least 30 home runs for nine consecutive seasons from 1953-61.

47 The 21-year-old third baseman set a Major League record in 1953 when he led the league with (47) home runs—at the time it was the highest total in history by a third baseman. So much for a sophomore slump—he also batted .302 with 135 RBIs. After Mathews hit another 40 home runs in only 138 games in 1954, baseball legend Ty Cobb said, "I've only known three or four perfect swings in my time. This lad has one of them."

493 Mathews' 500th home run came vs. Juan Marichal of the San Francisco Giants on July 14, 1967—exactly one year to the day earlier than Hank Aaron joined the 500 Home Run Club. Mathews was just the seventh player in history to reach that plateau, but he didn't get his milestone home run as a member of the Braves. He'd been traded to the Astros prior to 1967 after hitting (493) career bombs for the Braves franchise. A two-time home run champion in Milwaukee, Mathews' home run total remains the second highest in franchise history.

863 Eddie Mathews and Hank Aaron combined to hit a Major League record (863) home runs as teammates from 1954-66. In that span, they also combined to win five home run titles. The previous record was 859, set by Yankee teammates Lou Gehrig and Babe Ruth.

Warren Spahn

2 Warren Spahn said, "Hitting is timing. Pitching is upsetting timing." And Spahn is one of the greatest ever at upsetting timing. There are many examples that illustrate this point but the (2) no-hitters he tossed during his career make a pretty strong argument. They came in back-to-back seasons: on September 16, 1960 vs. Philadelphia and on April 28, 1961 vs. San Francisco. Spahn remains the only player in history to pitch a pair of no-nos for the Braves— and they actually came in a span of seven starts. His 1960 gem was at the end of the season—he made just three more starts—and his 1961 no-hitter was only his third start of the season.

5 The first recipient of the Cy Young Award was Don Newcombe in 1956. It was the Major League Cy Young Award at the time, rather than one award for each league. Warren Spahn was 20-11 that season, but that was only good enough to garner one vote in the balloting. In 1957, Spahn became the second recipient of the Major League Cy Young Award after posting a 21-11 record. That same season he led the league in wins for the fourth time in his career, but it was also the first of (5) *consecutive* seasons from 1957-61 that he'd post the highest wins total in the league. He never won the Cy Young again, but in that same span of five seasons he placed second in Cy Young balloting three times.

13 Warren Spahn and Christy Mathewson (New York Giants) share a NL record (13) seasons with 20 or more wins. Cy Young is the only player in history to surpass that total with a Major League record 15 seasons of 20 or more wins. However, Spahn is the only player in baseball history to lead the league in wins eight times. Young (5) and Mathewson (4) don't come close—and no one else has ever led the league in wins more than six times.

21 The jersey number (21) retired in honor of Warren Spahn. Inducted into the Hall of Fame in 1973, Spahn signed with the Braves fresh out of high school in 1940. His contract paid him $150. He appeared in four games in 1942, but did not return to the big leagues again until 1946 due to military service in Europe. Spahn, who joined the Army, fought in the Battle of the Bulge and was awarded both a Purple Heart and the Bronze Star for bravery.

363 Like many players of his era, Spahn gave up three years of his career to serve his country—and despite that, he still won (363) games. His first year back he was 8-5, but in 1947 the now 26-year-old lefty notched his first 20-win season, posting a 21-10 record and leading the league with a 2.33 earned run average. That began an extraordinary stretch in which Spahn won 20 or more games 13 times in 17 seasons from 1947-63. Spahn later said, "People say that my absence from the big leagues may have cost me a chance to win 400 games. But I don't know about that. I matured a lot in three years and I think I was better equipped to handle Major League hitters at 25 than I was at 22. Also, I pitched until I was 44. Maybe I wouldn't have been able to do that otherwise."

Dale Murphy

3 The jersey number (3) retired in honor of Dale Murphy. He was the Braves #1 and the fifth overall pick in the 1974 draft ... as a catcher. It was Bobby Cox who moved Murphy to the outfield in 1980. The move paid huge dividends in the field and at the plate—Murphy was a five-time Gold Glove winner, a two-time league MVP, and during the ten-year span from 1981-90 he hit more home runs and had more RBIs than any other player in baseball.

4 In baseball history there have been just (4) outfielders that have won league MVP honors in back-to-back seasons. Mickey Mantle did it in 1956-57, Roger Maris did it in 1960-61, and Dale Murphy did it in 1982-83. Barry Bonds later achieved this feat in 1992-93, and then again when he won the award four consecutive seasons from 2001-04. It's widely noted that among players currently eligible for the Hall of Fame, Maris and Murphy are the only two-time MVP recipients *not* enshrined at Cooperstown. In a previous book I argued Maris should be in the Hall of Fame—here I'd simply point out that during his prime, Murphy was the best player in the game. You can argue that his prime didn't last long enough or that his career numbers aren't strong enough, but then he didn't cheat either.

44 He hit (44) home runs in 1987 for a career high, but was second in the league behind a resurgent Andre Dawson, who blasted 49 for the Chicago Cubs. It also capped a remarkable run during which Murphy hit 30-plus home runs six times in eight seasons from 1980-87. The two seasons he failed to reach 30 home runs were 1981 and 1986. In 1981 the season was shortened due to the players' strike and he played just 104 games, and in 1986 he came up one short, hitting 29 bombs.

398 Murphy hit (398) career home runs. A two-time home run champion, his career total still ranks among the top 75 in baseball history. When he played his final game on May 21, 1993, his total was the 19th highest in MLB history. In terms of team history, you'll find him all over the franchise leader boards ... 1,926 games (fourth),

7,098 at bats (fourth), 1,103 runs (sixth), 1,901 hits (sixth), 3,394 total bases (fourth), 306 doubles (fifth), 371 home runs (fourth), 1,143 RBIs (fourth), 714 extra-base hits (fifth), and 2,841 times on base (fourth).

740 He also played in (740) consecutive games from September 26, 1981 through July 8, 1986. At the time it was the longest active streak in Major League baseball and the 11th longest in baseball history. During his streak, which now ranks as the 13th longest in history, he played in all 162 games on the Braves schedule four consecutive seasons from 1982-85. That stretch includes his back-to-back MVP seasons (1982-83), and it also includes back-to-back RBI titles (1982-83), back-to-back home run titles (1984-85), back-to-back seasons leading the league in slugging (1983-84), and a league best 118 runs in 1985.

Chipper Jones

10 The jersey number (10) the Braves will one day retire in honor of Chipper Jones. I can remember reading an article in a sports magazine as a kid, and the author was giving odds on who among current ballplayers would one day make it to the Hall of Fame. When he got to Dale Murphy, he simply wrote: "Dale Murphy will be in the Hall of Fame." Well, I'm going to take that same approach here: Chipper Jones will be in the Hall of Fame. The #1 overall pick in the 1990 draft, Chipper will be remembered as the greatest switch-hitting third baseman in baseball history. Greg Maddux was asked once about how he would pitch to Chipper. Maddux said, "I don't know. I'd come up with something. I could always walk him and try and pick him off. That's always a good way to go." Hal McRae, who managed in Tampa when the club was still the Devil Rays, once said of Chipper, "He hits the fastball from either side of the plate, he'll take walks, he doesn't over swing, and he wants to be at the plate with the game on the line. That's basically what you're looking for with any superstar."

John Smoltz

29 The jersey number (29) the Braves will one day retire in honor of John Smoltz. Maddux in 2009 … Glavine in 2010 … Cox in 2011 … Smoltzie in 2012? It's not if, but when. And with his resume, the same is true for Cooperstown. An eight-time All-Star, Cy Young recipient, and Rolaids Relief Man of the Year winner, he is the only pitcher in Major League history with 200 wins, 150 saves, and 3,000 strikeouts. He's the franchise leader for saves and strikeouts, and he's fifth in wins. Then you have to consider his postseason success: 15-4, four saves, 2.67 earned run average, 209 innings, and 199 strikeouts. Only Andy Pettitte (19) has won more postseason games, and Pettitte (263) and Tom Glavine (218) are the only pitchers with more postseason innings. No one has more postseason strikeouts than Smoltz—and no active players are even close. Smoltz will be eligible for the Hall of Fame in 2015, but when asked if he thinks about that he replied, "It doesn't bother me. People talk to me about that all the time, but I'm not consumed by it. My answer matches the way that I approach life: if it happens, great, and if it doesn't, it's not going to change me."

Greg Maddux

31 The jersey number (31) retired in honor of Greg Maddux. He was the sixth player to have his number retired by the Braves and the club wasted no time, inducting him into the Braves Hall of Fame and retiring his number on July 17, 2009, less than a year after his final game as a player. Maddux won three Cy Young Awards during 11 seasons with the club. Bobby Cox said the following as the Braves honored Maddux: "I get asked by managers and press people all the time, how good was he? Was he the best pitcher I ever saw? Was he the smartest pitcher I ever saw? Was he the best competitor I ever saw? The answer is yes to all the above." John Schuerholz, who signed Maddux after the 1992 season and brought him to Atlanta, answered those same questions this way, "No doubt, no question."

In the pregame ceremony Schuerholz pointed to the #31 jersey and said, "Now Greg, it's yours forever."

Tom Glavine

47 The jersey number (47) retired in honor of Tom Glavine. The biggest victory of his Hall of Fame career was Game 6 of the 1995 World Series. That was just one of the many memories that fans, players, and coaches were reminiscing about on August 6, 2010, when Glavine was honored during a pregame ceremony. Bobby Cox said one of Glavine's greatest attributes was his toughness. "He was as tough as it got," said Cox. "He pitched with injuries, pain. It was always good to know that Tommy was the guy pitching after you had lost two or three in a row. I've got all the respect in the world for how courageous he was, how competitive." Well, the next chapter for Glavine is no different than it is for Cox, Chipper, Smoltz, and Maddux ... they were the stars for one of the greatest teams ever assembled in baseball history, and they'll be immortalized as such at Cooperstown.

Francisco Cabrera

254 The career batting average (.254) during parts of five Major League seasons for Francisco Cabrera—which proves that it takes only one big hit, on the right stage, to become a legend. Cabrera is still honored in Atlanta, and rightfully so, for winning the 1992 NLCS vs. Pittsburgh.

"He might be the best 20-year-old rookie to ever play."
— Brian McCann, when asked about rookie teammate Jason Heyward

4 THE ROOKIES

THE ATLANTA BRAVES drafted Bob Horner as the #1 overall pick in 1978 out of Arizona State University. He was a 20-year-old slugger who'd just finished his junior year of college. He'd already hit 58 collegiate home runs and won numerous awards and honors, including MVP of the 1977 College World Series, but in terms of making headlines he was just getting started.

Horner began his career with the Atlanta Braves, as in that was the first stop on his professional journey—no time in the minors, not then, not ever. He went straight from ASU to the Atlanta Braves, and made his big league debut on June 16, 1978. And he didn't disappoint. That same year he was the National League's top rookie. Horner was the fourth member of the Braves to win that honor, and three others have since joined him, bringing the total to seven Braves who have been the league's top rookie. The numbers that follow tell their stories, and the rookie season stories of other notable names in franchise history.

Brett Butler

9 The number of steals (9) for Brett Butler during his 1981 rookie season with the Braves. The speedy outfielder was only caught stealing once that season—and in 40 games he scored 17 runs and batted .254. It was a good start for what would become a fantastic career. Butler played 89 games in 1982, but struggled, batting just .217. He bounced back in 1983, his final and only full season with the Braves, scoring 84 runs, stealing 39 bases, and leading the league with 13 triples. Unfortunately, the Braves traded Butler to Cleveland in a deal that brought Len Barker to Atlanta—and the speedy prospect went on to superstardom. Butler scored 90-plus runs in each of the next eight seasons—six times in that stretch he topped 100 runs—and he stole 30 or more bases the next ten seasons. Barker was 10-20 in parts of three seasons pitching for the Braves …

Bruce Benedict

11 Bruce Benedict gunned down (11) of 27 base runners attempting to steal against him during 22 games in 1978—his first season of big league action. That's not bad, throwing out 41% of would-be base stealers, especially for a 22-year-old rookie. Benedict was a fifth-round pick of the Braves in 1976 and he made his debut in August 1978. Benedict never developed as an offensive threat—hitting just .242 with 18 home runs during parts of 12 big league seasons—but he spent his entire career in Atlanta and was a valued member of the team from the very beginning because the pitching staff respected his leadership and defensive ability behind the plate.

Chipper Jones

11 Chipper Jones and the Braves made the postseason (11) consecutive seasons to begin his career. From 1995-2005, Chipper and the Braves made the same number of trips to the postseason as they did to spring training—a feat so rare, the odds against it are astronomical. Yet, it happened—and it did so in large part due to Chipper. He won at every level—high school, minors, and then in Atlanta. It was talent, yes, but it was also an attitude, a belief that he was supposed to win at every level. In spring training prior to his 1995 rookie season, Chipper was already so confident in who he was as a player that he famously deadpanned to veteran slugger Fred McGriff, after the Crime Dog grounded into an inning-ending double play, these two words: "Rally killer." His confidence carried over to the field, just as it had since he began playing as a kid—he batted .265, and he led all rookies with 23 home runs, 87 runs, and 86 RBIs. Hideo Nomo was Rookie of the Year for the Dodgers, but Chipper and the Braves were World Champions.

Darrell Evans

12 Darrell Evans hit (12) home runs during his 1971 rookie season with the Braves. He'd played 24 games and batted 70 times during call-ups in 1969-70, but he didn't hit his first big league homer until May 29, 1971. Who'd he go yard against for the first time? None other than Hall of Fame legend Bob Gibson ... and speaking of the Hall of Fame, with 414 career home runs it's a shame that Evans has never been given more consideration for Cooperstown. Bill James once said that Evans is absolutely "the most underrated player in baseball history." He wasn't underrated in Atlanta—his slick defense and big stick was much appreciated in the city where he developed as a player and hit 131 home runs. In the category of Darrell Evans trivia ... he was the first player in baseball history to hit 40-plus home runs in both leagues, and he was the second player in history (behind Reggie Jackson) to hit 100-plus home runs with three different teams (Braves, Giants, Tigers).

Ernie Johnson

15 Long before his legendary broadcast career, Ernie Johnson Sr. posted a 2-0 record during (15) relief appearances in his 1950 rookie season pitching for the Boston Braves. He earned his first big league win pitching vs. the New York Giants at the Polo Grounds on June 30, 1950. Johnson started only 19 games in his career, but he was an outstanding reliever. In 1952, his first full season with the Braves, Johnson was 6-3 while pitching in 29 games. He went on to make 224 relief appearances during eight seasons with the Braves, easily the most on the team during that span—and he was a key member of the pitching staff during the 1957 World Championship season.

Vinny Castilla

21 Vinny Castilla played (21) games for the Braves during call-ups in 1991-92. The slugger was a valued prospect, but he was only 5 for 21 with no home runs during that time. In November 1992, the Colorado Rockies selected Castilla in the expansion draft—so of course he developed into the slugger everyone had expected him to be in the first place. Castilla hit 320 career home runs, including 239 for the Rockies. He had an amazing five-year run for Colorado from 1995-99, hitting 32, 40, 40, 46, and 33 home runs in those seasons— but oddly enough, he never led the league in homers. Castilla finally came back to the Braves as a free agent, playing third base for the club and temporarily moving Chipper Jones to left field in 2002-03. In those two seasons, Castilla, now a veteran, combined for 34 home runs.

David Justice

28 David Justice made his big league debut on May 24, 1989, but played in only 16 games that season. It wasn't until 1990 that he became a Braves' regular—and only then after starting the season at Richmond. He rejoined the Braves on May 16, and all he did was hit safely in his first ten games, and 14 out of 15 overall. Justice batted .350 in that span with two home runs, but he was just getting started in terms of power. He was eighth in the league with (28) home runs despite playing only 127 games. His home run total was second on the club behind Ron Gant and tops in the league among rookies, but it was his late summer power surge that got the attention of everyone in baseball. Justice homered eight times total from May through July, but in August alone he batted .301 with 11 home runs and 29 RBIs, earning Player of the Month honors for the National League. His hot hitting continued in September and October, as he batted .330 with nine home runs and 21 RBIs during the season's final 31 games to wrap up top rookie honors.

Earl Williams

33 The Braves first-round pick in 1965, Earl Williams set an Atlanta era record when he hit (33) home runs as a 22-year-old rookie in 1971. His home run total was fifth highest in the league, and he also batted .260 with 87 RBIs in 145 games to easily win Rookie of the Year honors. Williams was traded to the Baltimore Orioles after hitting 28 home runs in his sophomore season, but after his numbers slipped the next two seasons he was traded back to Atlanta in 1975. Unfortunately he never regained the same form he displayed in 1971-72, and after bouncing around to a couple other teams he was released for good on May 17, 1978.

Samuel Jethroe

35 Samuel "Jet" Jethroe led the National League with (35) steals during his 1950 rookie campaign. In 141 games he also scored 100 runs and hit 18 home runs and for his performance he was awarded Rookie of the Year honors. Jet was an anomaly of sorts, because he was a 33-year-old rookie outfielder. He'd had a tryout once with the Boston Red Sox, along with Jackie Robinson and Marvin Williams, but none were offered contracts—so instead, he continued to star in the Negro Leagues where he consistently posted high averages, stole a ridiculous number of bases, and played for winning teams. By the time he finally made his big league debut for the Braves on April 18, 1950, he'd already played a full career's worth of games in the Negro Leagues. His Major League career lasted just three full seasons, during which he led the league in steals in back-to-back seasons and was second in steals during his third and final season.

Rafael Furcal

40 Rafael Furcal made the jump from Class A ball to the Major Leagues in 2000 after Braves shortstop Walt Weiss suffered an injury. In 131 games, Furcal batted .295 with 87 runs and a team high (40) steals—also the fifth highest steals total in the league. Furcal beat out the likes of Rick Ankiel, Pat Burrell, Lance Berkman, and Juan Pierre to win league Rookie of the Year honors. Furcal stole 189 bases in six seasons with the Braves, good for the tenth highest total in franchise history. He was also on the Braves' postseason roster five times, stealing nine additional bases in 22 playoff games—unfortunately, the Braves lost all five Division Series' that Furcal played in. Furcal was actually on the losing end of the first six postseason series' he played. It wasn't until the Dodgers beat the Cubs during the 2008 Division Series that he tasted postseason success. In 2011, in his ninth career trip to the postseason, Furcal got the ultimate success, playing for the World Champion St. Louis Cardinals.

Craig Kimbrel

46 Craig Kimbrel established a Major League rookie record with (46) saves in 2011. The All-Star saved 27 games prior to the All-Star break, also a rookie record, and was the NL Rookie of the Month twice—in June and August. Kimbrel was perfect in ten save opportunities in August and established yet another Major League record when he struck out at least two batters in ten consecutive appearances during which he pitched an inning or less. The previous record was seven such appearances, first set by Matt Mantei (1999) tied by Billy Wagner (2007), and oddly enough, tied by ... Kimbrel, during call-ups in 2010 when his record-tying seven appearances were spread over June, August, and September. In his full-fledged rookie season in 2011, Kimbrel won Rookie of the Year honors in a unanimous vote. The last player to win the award in such fashion was Albert Pujols in 2001.

Jeff Blauser

88 Jeff Blauser was the Braves #1 pick and the overall #5 pick in the 1984 draft. Blauser made his big league debut as a pinch-hitter for Doyle Alexander on July 5, 1987, hitting a ground out to Cardinals' shortstop Ozzie Smith. Blauser didn't pick up his first big league hit until August 12, more than a month later, but just four days after that he smacked his first big league home run and Braves' fans got a glimpse of why Blauser was such a highly valued prospect: he was a middle infielder who could hit *bombs*. Blauser became the Braves everyday shortstop two years later. He hit 12 home runs that season—and hit double digits in seven of nine seasons as the Braves starter, including ten in 1996, despite being limited to only 83 games due to injuries. Blauser bounced back and hit a career high 17 home runs and made his second All-Star team in 1997, his final season with the club. All total he hit 122 career home runs, 109 home runs for the Braves, and (88) home runs as the Braves shortstop—the highest total for any shortstop in franchise history.

Bob Horner

89 It took Bob Horner only (89) games to earn Rookie of the Year honors in 1978. The 20-year-old third baseman jumped straight from college to the pros and hit 23 home runs in just 323 at bats. His first game was on June 16 and he batted in the sixth hole, behind catcher Dale Murphy. Horner wasted little time proving he belonged—in his third at bat he blasted a long two-run home run against Hall of Famer Bert Blyleven. Horner was plagued by injuries throughout his career, however, leaving fans to wonder what his numbers could have been if he'd stayed healthy. He was, after all, limited to just ten years in the big leagues—but years later when he was asked about this, Horner answered, "I had a great time and I lived a dream. I wouldn't trade it for anything in the world … my regret is that you have a couple of injuries and it cuts short a couple of things you'd like to have done, but when you start going down that road it serves no purpose. It is what it is."

Andruw Jones

113 Andruw Jones made the Braves' 1996 postseason roster despite the fact he'd made just (113) *career* plate appearances. The 19-year-old outfielder batted .217 with five home runs during 31 games for the Braves after making his debut on August 15. Jones homered vs. St. Louis in the NLCS, making him the youngest player in history to hit a postseason home run. In the World Series vs. New York, Jones became just the second player in history to homer in his first two World Series at bats—and he did it at Yankee Stadium. Jones was only fifth in Rookie of the Year balloting … *in 1997*, his official rookie season, and one year *after* he'd starred for the Braves in the postseason.

Glenn Hubbard

258 The batting average (.258) for 20-year-old second baseman Glenn Hubbard during 44 games in 1978—his first year wearing a Braves uniform. Hubbard was only a 20th-round draft pick in 1975, but then he was also a 17-year-old kid fresh out of high school. And despite not being a top tier pick, he reached the majors very quickly. It took only two full seasons in the minors before he got his first taste of big league action on July 14, 1978—but then, in 1978, Hubbard was producing at AAA Richmond as if he'd been the #1 overall pick in 1975 ... in only 80 games he batted .336 with 101 hits, 12 doubles, three triples, 14 home runs, 58 runs, and 36 RBIs. He was up and down with the club from 1978-80, finally taking over the starting job for the Braves in 1981.

Javy Lopez

277 After 17 appearances during call-ups in 1992-93, Javy Lopez hit 13 home runs in only (277) at bats during his 1994 rookie season. He played 80 games that year, but his powerful bat earned him more and more playing time over guys like Charlie O'Brien and Eddie Perez until he finally emerged as the Braves everyday catcher and a bona fide superstar. Lopez hit 214 career home runs for the Braves. That total is eighth highest in franchise history, and he hit 209 of them as a catcher—easily a franchise record.

Freddie Freeman

282 Freddie Freeman led all Braves' starters with a (.282) batting average in 2011. Not bad for a rookie. Then again, this is the kid who hit his first big league bomb against none other than Roy Halladay ...

the same kid whose leather at first is so flashy than at times it's hard to decide which to be more excited about, his bat or his glove, the same kid who joined teammate Dan Uggla with concurrent 20-game hitting streaks in 2011—a first in modern era Braves' history—and the same kid who won NL Rookie of the Month honors in July after hitting .362 with six homers, 17 runs, and 18 RBIs. If not for teammate Craig Kimbrel, Freeman would have easily won Rookie of the Year honors. Instead, he finished second. It was the first time since Gene Conley and Hank Aaron in 1954 that two players finished in the top five in Rookie of the Year balloting for the Braves, and the first time any two teammates finished first and second since Jerome Walton and Dwight Smith did it for the Chicago Cubs in 1989.

Ron Gant

321 Ron Gant made his Major League debut for the Braves as a 22-year-old second baseman on September 6, 1987. A powerful hitter, he later made the transition to the outfield and enjoyed a successful career in which he hit (321) regular season home runs—including 147 for the Braves—and another eight bombs in the postseason. No matter how many bombs you hit, though, you never forget the first one ... especially in this case. It took 12 games before Gant finally connected for his first big league blast, but the guy on the mound when Gant went yard ... Nolan Ryan. For a kid getting his first cup of coffee in the big leagues, it must have felt surreal.

Alvin Dark

322 In 1948 the phrase "Spahn and Sain and two days of rain" was frequently used around the ballpark, but in addition to the dynamic pitching duo the Pennant-winning Braves had some help from a rookie shortstop. Alvin Dark was fourth in the league with a (.322) batting average, second best on the team behind outfielder Tommy Holmes (.325). Jackie Robinson was the first recipient of the Major League Rookie of the Year Award in 1947, and Alvin Dark became the second player to receive the award in 1948. Dark played only one more season in Boston before being traded to the New York Giants, where he played on two more Pennant-winning teams and was a member of the World Series Champion 1954 Giants.

Jason Heyward

393 The J-Hey Kid posted an impressive (.393) on-base percentage during his 2010 rookie season. He was baseball's top-rated rookie that year and wasted no time living up to the hype. His batting practice home runs in spring training were traveling so far that he was doing damage to vehicles in a parking lot that previously had been considered a "safe" distance from batted balls. In his first big league at bat he hit a three-run home run that traveled more than 470 feet. But it wasn't just his power that impressed, it was his discipline at the plate—Heyward was fourth in the league in walks (91) and fourth in the league in on-base percentage, numbers that are almost unheard of for rookies. He lost a close vote for Rookie of the Year honors, placing second behind Buster Posey of the Giants.

Kevin Millwood

403 The earned run average (4.03) for 22-year-old rookie Kevin Millwood in 1997. He made his big league debut that season on July 14, tossing two scoreless innings in relief vs. Philly to earn his first career victory. Millwood's next four appearances came as a starter, and he struggled, losing three of four as his ERA ballooned to 5.48. However, beginning on August 30, Millwood ran off a string of three straight victories in a span of four starts to close out his rookie campaign with a 5-3 record. His strong pitching down the stretch wasn't enough to earn a spot on the postseason roster, but it was more than enough to earn him a serious look for 1998—and he took full advantage of it, earning a spot in the Braves' rotation. Millwood responded with a 17-8 record during his first full season in the majors, and in a five-year span from 1998-2002 he posted totals of 17, 18, 10, 7, and 18 victories. All total, Millwood was 75-46 during five-plus seasons with the Braves.

Kelly Johnson

417 Kelly Johnson was a rookie in 2005 when he won National League Player of the Week honors for the first time. He batted (.417) from June 13-19, including three home runs and 11 RBIs. As for his three home runs ... they were also the first three of his career, and one of them was a grand slam. In that same game, Johnson was just the fourth rookie to tally six RBIs in a game for Atlanta. Johnson had made his debut on May 29, but began his career 0 for 15 ... no worries though, as he raised his average .177 points in that remarkable seven-game stretch in June.

Martin Prado

462 Martin Prado began the 2006 season at Double-A Mississippi but was promoted to the big club and made his Major League debut on April 23. He was 1 for 2 with two walks, and his first hit with the Braves was a triple. Unlike McCann, Heyward, and Freeman, Prado was up and down between the Braves and the minors for three seasons before finally playing his way into a starting role after replacing an injured Kelly Johnson in 2009. However, during his frequent and sometimes brief call-ups he made the most of every opportunity as illustrated by his (.462) batting average with runners in scoring position during the 24 games he played for the Braves in 2006. He was 6 for 13 with RISP, including a three-run home run against Jamie Moyer on September 14—the first of his big league career—that led the Braves to a 4-1 victory.

Brian McCann

563 The slugging percentage (.563) for Brian McCann during the 2005 Division Series vs. Houston. The 21-year-old rookie catcher made his big league debut on June 10, 2005, and saw action in 59 regular season games, during which he batted .278 with 5 home runs. In the postseason, however, he was clearly unfazed by October baseball. In Game 2 of the Division Series, McCann hit a three-run home run in the first postseason at bat of his career. He was the first player in franchise history to accomplish that feat—and he did it against Roger Clemens, no less. McCann finished the series with two homers and five RBIs in three games. His play as a rookie was so solid that the Braves traded Johnny Estrada to Arizona and named McCann the starting catcher in 2006, and all he's done since then is make six consecutive All-Star teams.

Tommy Hanson

733 The winning percentage (.733) for Tommy Hanson during his 2009 rookie season. He was the consensus #1 prospect in baseball that season, and it didn't take him long to live up to the hype, either. After earning a no-decision in his June 7 debut, Hanson reeled off five consecutive victories in his next seven starts—including wins vs. the New York Yankees and the Boston Red Sox. Hanson finished the season 11-4 with a 2.89 earned run average in only 21 starts. He was third in Rookie of the Year balloting.

"My mother used to pitch to me and my father would shag balls. If I hit one up the middle close to my mother, I'd have some extra chores to do. My mother was instrumental in making me a pull hitter."
— *Eddie Mathews, Hall of Fame Induction Speech*

5 THE SLUGGERS

THE ATLANTA BRAVES career leader in slugging percentage is Hank Aaron … no surprise there. After all, Aaron led the league in slugging four times and led the league in home runs four times—and only two of those seasons overlapped, meaning twice Aaron led the league in home runs but not slugging, and twice he led the league in slugging, but not home runs. By any reasonable standard (*i.e. he didn't cheat*), Aaron is one of the greatest sluggers in baseball history—and there shouldn't even be a debate about who is baseball's true all-time home run champion (*again, no cheating*).

Aaron, of course, isn't the only slugger to suit it up for the Braves. What follows is a look at the Braves' top ten career leaders in slugging percentage … by the numbers. And then we take a look at numbers for other players who had some monstrous seasons.

Eddie Mathews

3 On September 27, 1952, 20-year-old rookie Eddie Mathews hit (3) home runs vs. Brooklyn in an 11-3 victory, the last ever for the Braves in Boston. The following day, Boston and Brooklyn tied, 5-5, and the following season the Braves moved to Milwaukee. As for Mathews, he was the first rookie in Major League history to hit three home runs in a single game. His strong finish gave him 25 home runs and a .447 slugging percentage for the season, but that was nothing compared to what he did from 1953-55. The next three seasons, Mathews hit 47, 40, and 41 home runs, with slugging percentages of .627, .603, and .601. In 17 big league seasons, Mathews slugged .509 overall, but never led the league in slugging in any one season. Despite that, his career slugging percentage is among the top 100 in baseball history—and his .517 career mark with the Braves remains the fifth highest in franchise history.

Joe Adcock

18 Joe Adcock set a Major League record that lasted nearly five decades when he totaled (18) bases in a single game vs. Brooklyn on July 31, 1954. He did it on the strength of four home runs, becoming just the seventh player in history with a four-homer game. Adcock's finest season with the Braves was 1956. In only 137 games he batted .291 with 103 RBIs, and he set career highs with 38 home runs and a .597 slugging percentage. Adcock never led the league in homers or slugging, but he finished his career with 336 home runs—which still ranks among the top 100 in baseball history—and his .511 slugging percentage during ten seasons with the Braves remains the eighth highest in franchise history.

Wally Berger

38 Earl Williams hit 33 home runs as a rookie in 1971—that's the record for the Atlanta era of franchise history—but the record for all eras was set in 1930 when Wally Berger hit (38) home runs as a 24-year-old outfielder in his first big league season. Berger was third in the league in home runs, sixth in the league with 79 extra-base hits, and eighth in the league with a .614 slugging percentage. Not a bad start to his career, to say the least. Berger's stats, however, would be the highest of his career, despite the fact he later won a home run title (34, in 1935). Berger never led the league in slugging percentage, but in seven seasons with the Braves from 1930-36 he was among the league's top ten leaders five times—including a second, third, and fourth in successive seasons. Berger was the franchise leader in slugging percentage until Hank Aaron came along, but his career .533 mark remains the second best in franchise history.

Fred McGriff

51 On July 20, 1993, Fred McGriff played his first game as a member of the Braves. Atlanta began play that day trailing the Giants by nine games, but the Braves were about to catch fire ... literally. McGriff joined the lineup and the Braves press box at Atlanta-Fulton County Stadium famously caught fire prior to the game. Once play began, the Braves fell behind early against the Cardinals, trailing 5-0 in the sixth inning—but Jeff Blauser hit a three-run homer, and two batters later Fred McGriff hit a game-tying two-run shot, and the Braves went on to rally for an 8-5 victory. Atlanta won (51) games after acquiring McGriff, losing just 17, and overcame a ten-game deficit to win a third straight Division Title. The Crime Dog batted .310 in 68 games, belting 19 home runs with 55 RBIs, and his slugging percentage was .612. McGriff's best season was cut short due to the 1994 work stoppage. In only 113 games he'd already hit 34 home runs with 94 RBIs—with a career high .623 slugging percentage. A two-time home run champion, McGriff never led the league in slugging, but in five seasons with the Braves he posted a .516 slugging percentage—the sixth highest in franchise history.

Andruw Jones

78 The number of extra-base hits (78) for Andruw Jones in 2000 and 2005. That total was the tenth best in the league in 2000, and the fourth best in 2005, but it is also tied for the tenth highest season total in franchise history. In 2000, Jones slugged .541, and in 2005 he slugged a career high .575 that was fifth best in the league. Jones slugged .497 during his career with the Braves, which is among the top 15 in franchise history—but his 368 home runs and 732 extra-base hits for the Braves are both among the five highest totals in franchise history.

Del Crandall

170 Del Crandall hit (170) home runs during 13 seasons with the Boston and Milwaukee Braves. The catcher had 15-plus home runs during eight consecutive seasons from 1953-60, including a career high 26 in 1955 when he also set a career high with a .474 slugging percentage. Crandall, who was an eight-time All-Star, held the franchise record for home runs by a catcher until he was surpassed by Javy Lopez in April 2003—but his 170 career home runs remains the tenth highest total in franchise history.

Felipe Alou

355 The number of total bases (355) for Felipe Alou in 1966. The first baseman / outfielder batted a career high .327 on the strength of a league best 218 hits. He also had 32 doubles, six triples, and 31 home runs to lead the league in total bases. Alou only placed fifth in league MVP balloting, despite having statistically one of the best offensive seasons in franchise history. With 69 extra-base hits, Alou also slugged a career high .533, and his 355 total bases remains one of the ten best season totals in franchise history.

Freddie Freeman

448 The slugging percentage (.448) for Freddie Freeman during his 2011 rookie season. The powerful first baseman batted .282, and he hit 32 doubles and 21 home runs. Freeman slugged .521 twice in the minors—with Class A Rome in 2008 (18 homers in 130 games) and again with AAA Gwinnett in 2010 (18 homers in 124 games). In July 2011, he was a one-man wrecking crew, slugging .600 for the month and leaving fans salivating over his potential in the future—after all, he'll only be 22 as he begins 2012 ...

Herman Long

474 The number of extra-base hits (474) for Herman Long during 13 seasons with the Braves. Long was a shortstop who stood 5' 8" in his spikes, yet he legged out 295 doubles, 91 triples, and 88 home runs for his career. He slugged .505 in 1894 for a career high, and he also set a career high with 12 home runs. Long actually won a home run title with the Braves in 1900—he hit 12 that season, too. His career .390 slugging percentage with the Braves isn't even among the club's top 50, but his 474 extra-base hits is the seventh highest total in franchise history, ranking ahead of big names such as Joe Adcock, Javy Lopez, and Bob Horner.

David Justice

499 The slugging percentage (.499) for David Justice during parts of eight seasons with the Braves. Justice hit 160 regular season home runs for Atlanta, plus seven more in the postseason—including the most important bomb of his career in Game 6 of the 1995 World Series. He slugged .535 during his 1990 rookie season for his highest percentage with the Braves, but his best home run total, 40, came in 1993 along with a .515 slugging percentage. Oddly enough, especially for someone who was considered a slugger in his career, Justice ranks among the top 15 in franchise history for career slugging percentage, and yet none of his best seasons slugging with the Braves even make the top 50 season efforts in franchise history.

Jason Heyward

507 The minor league slugging percentage (.507) for Jason Heyward. The 2007 first-round draft pick slugged .555 in 2009—his third minor league season—hit 17 home runs in only 99 games, and was promoted from Class A Myrtle Beach, to AA Mississippi, to AAA Gwinnett in the course of one season. And the following season he was a 20-year-old rookie who slugged .456 for the Braves with 18 home runs in 142 games. The runner-up in 2010 Rookie of the Year balloting, Heyward slumped in his sophomore season as he dealt with various injuries—however, if he's healthy in 2012, watch out ...

Chipper Jones

533 The slugging percentage (.533) for Chipper Jones from 1993-2011. That ties him with Wally Berger for the second best percentage in franchise history as Chipper prepares for 2012. At times Chipper has surpassed Berger and been second all alone, at other times he's fallen below Berger into third—but he finished 2011 tied. With the exception of Hank Aaron, however, Chipper's slugging percentage is easily the most impressive in franchise history. Chipper's first big league game was in 1993, after all—his longevity alone makes his career slugging percentage a staggering statistic. He's topped .600 in slugging three times with a career high .633 when he hit 45 home runs in his 1999 MVP season. Oddly enough ... Chipper never led the league in slugging, and in fact, Chipper never led the league in *anything* until 2007, in his twelfth full big league season, when he posted a 1.029 on-base plus slugging percentage that was the best in the NL. Chipper did one better in 2008, winning the league batting title with a .364 average. In terms of slugging, despite never leading the league, Chipper's hallmark has been his consistency—in 11 of 13 seasons from 1996-2008, Chipper's slugging percentage was above .500.

Bob Horner

552 The slugging percentage (.552) for Bob Horner in 1979. The 21-year-old third baseman led the team in slugging during his sophomore season with the club. He was also fifth in the league in slugging after hitting .314 with 33 home runs. Horner led the club in slugging again in 1980, and this time he was second in the league with a .529 slugging percentage. He would be among the league's top ten leaders in slugging only two more times—in 1982 and 1985—but he posted a .500-plus slugging percentage five times in his first six big league seasons. After nine seasons with the Braves, he left with a career .508 slugging percentage, the fifth highest in franchise history at the time. Today, Horner's career mark remains the ninth best for the Braves.

Andruw Jones

575 The slugging percentage (.575) for Andruw Jones in 2005. It was one of the greatest slugging seasons in franchise history, as Jones established a new franchise record with a league best 51 home runs. He also led the league with 128 RBIs, was second in league MVP balloting, made his fourth All-Star team, won his eighth consecutive Gold Glove, and took home his first Silver Slugger Award. Jones narrowly lost the MVP to Albert Pujols.

Tommy Holmes

577 The league leading slugging percentage (.577) for Tommy Holmes in 1945. The Boston outfielder had one of the greatest offensive seasons in franchise history, yet he placed second in MVP balloting to one of the least recognized MVP recipients in National League history—Phil Cavarretta, who won the batting title and hit six home runs that season for the Cubs. Holmes batted .352, losing the batting title by .003 percentage points, and he led the league with 224 hits, 47 doubles, and 28 home runs. Holmes was second in RBIs as well with 117, just seven off the league best 124 for Brooklyn's Dixie Walker. In other words, Holmes nearly won the Triple Crown. He also had 81 extra-base hits, which at the time was the highest total in franchise history during the post-1900 modern era, and the second highest behind Hugh Duffy's 85 in 1894. Today, his 81 extra-base hits remains the sixth best season total in franchise history. As for the rest of Holmes' career, he continued to hit for average, but he never hit more than nine home runs in any season after 1945, and his highest RBIs total was 79.

Dale Murphy

580 The slugging percentage (.580) for Dale Murphy in 1987. Murphy established career highs that season in both slugging and home runs. He was fifth in the league in slugging, and his 44 home runs were second behind Andre Dawson. Murphy led the league in slugging twice (1983-84), and from 1980-87 he slugged .500 or better six times. He was the game's most feared slugger in that time, and remains one of the greatest in franchise history.

Andres Galarraga

595 The slugging percentage (.595) for Andres Galarraga in 1998. In his first season with the Braves, the powerful first baseman led the club in slugging, home runs, and RBIs. Galarraga hit 44 bombs with 121 RBIs, and he also established a franchise record with *eight* multi-home run games.

Gary Sheffield

604 The slugging percentage (.604) for Gary Sheffield in 2003. He was a key part of a Braves offense that led the league in average, scoring, slugging, and home runs. Sheffield batted .330 with 39 home runs and 132 RBIs—but he was only third in MVP balloting, trailing Barry Bonds and Albert Pujols. Sheffield also banged out 78 extra-base hits in 2003, tying Andruw Jones' 2000 total for the tenth highest season effort in franchise history.

Wes Covington

622 The slugging percentage (.622) for Wes Covington in 1958. He batted .330 and slammed 24 home runs in only 90 games. The outfielder was ninth in the league in home runs and he led the Braves in slugging—which is saying something, since his teammates included Eddie Mathews, Hank Aaron, and Joe Adcock. At the time it was the seventh highest season slugging percentage in franchise history—and today it remains the tenth best.

Rogers Hornsby

632 Rogers Hornsby slugged (.632) for the Boston Braves in 1928. It was the Hall of Famer's only season with the Braves, and all he did was bat .387 with 21 home runs for a league best slugging percentage that remains the seventh best season effort in franchise history.

Javy Lopez

687 The slugging percentage (.687) for Javy Lopez during his monstrous 2003 season. He won his only career Silver Slugger Award that season, was an All-Star for the third time, and placed fifth in MVP balloting after setting career highs with a .328 average, 43 home runs, 89 runs, and 109 RBIs ... in only 129 games. Those are amazing stats for anyone, but for a catcher they're insanely ridiculous. His 43 home runs set a franchise record for catchers and his .687 slugging percentage is the highest for a Braves' player during the post-1900 modern era. Despite his gaudy numbers, Lopez was only fourth in the league in home runs and second in slugging behind Barry Bonds. It was the fourth time that Lopez slugged greater than .500 for the Braves—he'd also done it three consecutive seasons from 1997-99. When he left for Baltimore in 2004, he did so with a career .502 slugging percentage for the Braves—and that remains the tenth highest in franchise history.

Hugh Duffy

694 Hall of Fame legend Hugh Duffy won the Triple Crown in 1894 when he batted a Major League record .440 for the Boston Beaneaters with 237 hits in only 125 games, 18 home runs, 145 RBIs, a .502 on-base percentage, 374 total bases, and a (.694) slugging percentage—the best season effort in franchise history.

Ryan Klesko

875 Ryan Klesko was a 24-year-old outfielder in his second big league season when he belted 23 home runs in only 329 at bats in 1995. He batted .310 and 50 of his 102 hits went for extra-bases, good for a career high .608 slugging percentage. Klesko had been up with the Braves in 1992-93, and he'd hit 17 home runs in 92 games in 1994, but nothing he did during that span even came close to approaching the success he had during the 1995 postseason. In his first career playoff series, Klesko batted .467 vs. Colorado in the Division Series—and then against the Indians in the World Series, Klesko homered three times and had a (.875) slugging percentage. Klesko followed his breakthrough season with 34 home runs in 1996, a career high, and four times in six seasons with the Braves (1994-96, 1999) Klesko slugged .500 or better. When he left for San Diego in 2000, he did so with a .525 career slugging percentage—the fourth best in Braves' history.

Hank Aaron

1,477 Curt Simmons once said of Hank Aaron, "Trying to throw a fastball by Henry Aaron is like trying to sneak a sunrise past a rooster." Pretty good analogy, actually—because otherwise, there's no way for a player to slug a Major League record (1,477) extra-base hits … but that's exactly what Aaron did. He led the league in that category five times: 1959, 1961, 1963, 1967, and 1969. Aaron's 92 extra-base hits in 1959 set a career high—and no surprise, that same season he also led the league in slugging percentage for the first time. His .636 slugging percentage that season stood as his career high for more than a decade, but he actually eclipsed it in 1971. The 37-year-old veteran hit 47 home runs and led the league with a .669 slugging percentage, both career highs. Aaron's career slugging percentage is .555, one of the top 25 in baseball history—his slugging percentage with the Braves was .567, the absolute best in franchise history.

Adam LaRoche

1,657 Braves' first baseman Adam LaRoche is seventh in franchise history with a .512 slugging percentage during (1,657) career plate appearances with the club. That's the lowest total PA among the Braves' top ten leaders in slugging. From 2004-11, LaRoche slugged .478 overall with five different teams, which would have dropped him completely off the Braves' leader board if he'd been with the club that entire time. However, that's not to say LaRoche wasn't a true slugger with the Braves. He definitely was—belting 13 home runs as a platoon player during his 2004 rookie season, and then 20 home runs while still platooning in his 2005 sophomore season. His breakout season was 2006, when the lefty set career highs with 32 home runs and a .561 slugging percentage. LaRoche hit 20-plus home runs in six consecutive seasons from 2005-10, with 25-plus in four of those seasons.

"You go to Spring Training every year expecting to win."
— *Bobby Cox*

6 THE MANAGERS AND COACHES

THE ATLANTA BRAVES began a new era in 2011, taking the field for the first time since 1990 without Bobby Cox. Well, sort of. Cox was around so much in Spring Training that Chipper Jones, among other players, joked about their former skipper, saying, "There hasn't been a time that I've walked into Fredi's office that Bobby hasn't been in there." It wasn't a bad thing, though. After all, 2011 was the first time that Chipper took the field as a big league player without Bobby Cox in the dugout. Chipper added, "I think Bobby being here [Spring Training] and being around is a tremendous influence on Fredi and the rest of the coaching staff. He's a good man to have around."

Well, he is a good man to have around, for sure, but once the season began in earnest his absence also left some very big shoes to fill for new skipper Fredi Gonzalez. That didn't concern bench coach Carlos Tosca, who said, "From day one he always had a tremendous attitude, very upbeat. He was a smart player—the same thing he is as a manager. The one thing about Fredi is he is very consistent."

This new era began with a lot of optimism in Spring Training, but its first season came to a bitter end on the season's final day. The Braves failed to put away the Wild Card down the stretch, despite leading the Cardinals by 10.5 games on August 25. Atlanta lost 20 of 31 games to close the season, St. Louis won 23 of 32, and when the Braves lost the season finale to the Phillies, the Cardinals claimed the Wild Card.

And yet, disappointing as it was, you can be sure the Braves will break camp in 2012 with the same mindset Bobby Cox preached for the past 20 years—and the same approach that Fredi Gonzalez takes now—"expect to win."

What follows is a look at Bobby Cox, Fredi Gonzalez, and other big names that made an impact on Braves' history as managers or coaches, by the numbers.

Ted Turner

1 Ted Turner famously managed the Braves for (1) game in 1977. The Braves had lost 16 straight, so team owner Turner put on a No. 27 uni and suited it up for one game—unfortunately, his managerial career was short-lived and unsuccessful. The Braves lost 2-1, and Baseball Commissioner Bowie Kuhn ruled that anyone with ownership in a club could not also manage it, thus ending his "career" as a manager. Turner responded to Kuhn by saying, "If I'm smart enough to save $11 million to buy the team, I ought to be smart enough to manage it." Fredi Gonzalez might be the team's 47th manager, but that total includes Ted Turner and 19 others who managed the club for less than a year each—12 of those managers were on board for fewer than 100 games, mostly in an interim capacity, and two of them managed the club for only three games and one game respectively.

Brian Snitker

4 Brian Snitker's playing career lasted (4) minor league seasons in the

Braves organization. The catcher out of the University of New Orleans had been signed as an undrafted free agent, but four years later his playing career was over and a new one was set to begin, thanks to Hank Aaron. "I was fortunate when Hank offered me the coaching job," said Snitker. "I was single and living out of my car, so I gave it a try to see what happened." Including his four years playing in the minors, Snitker has now been part of the Braves family for 35 years. His first tour of duty with the big club was as the bullpen coach in 1985, and his second was in the same position from 1988-90. In the intervening years he was an instructor and manager in the Braves' farm system. "The players are the one thing that keeps you coming back," said Snitker. "And that's because we have good players. The Braves always get guys who are good people with strong work ethnics and great makeup. They have the intangibles that make them the best players they can be. And that's what makes it fun to go to work everyday." In 2012, Snitker will begin his sixth consecutive season as the Braves third base coach and his tenth overall season during three stints with the big club.

Carlos Tosca

6 Braves' bench coach Carlos Tosca was just the (6th) manager in history to lead a Major League team despite having *never* played a single game of professional baseball. He managed the Richmond Braves in 2001, and then joined the Blue Jays coaching staff in 2002. Blue Jays' manager Buck Martinez was fired on June 3, and that same day, Tosca won his managerial debut 6-1 vs. Tampa Bay. He spent three seasons leading the Blue Jays, managed 17 seasons in the minors, and was on staff for the inaugural Arizona Diamondbacks club. The 2012 season will be his second as bench coach for Fredi Gonzalez and the Braves. Just how remarkable is his story? Well, he graduated from the University of South Florida with a degree in Phys. Ed. in 1976 and got his first coaching job as a high school pitching coach. Not even the head coach, mind you—the *high school* pitching coach. And yet two years later he moved into the

professional ranks, and now 36 years later, he's embarking on his 13th season as a Major League coach.

Leo Mazzone

6 It's hard to find a number that speaks louder than this: (6) Cy Young Awards in an eight-year span from 1991-98. Tom Glavine (1991), Greg Maddux (1993-95), John Smoltz (1996), and Tom Glavine again (1998) ... without question, Leo Mazzone was one of the greatest pitching coaches in baseball. And it's not just the Cy Young Awards that lead to such an obvious conclusion—it's also guys like Denny Neagle (20-5, 1997), Russ Ortiz (21-7, 2003), and Jaret Wright (15-8, 2004) who thrived under Mazzone's guidance and then left Atlanta and never replicated that kind of success again (and it's not even close).

Casey Stengel

7 Casey Stengel won ten Pennants and managed (7) World Championship teams ... *after* six unsuccessful seasons managing the Braves. The Hall of Fame legend had just one winning season in Boston, and never placed higher than fifth in the standings from 1938-43. He didn't manage again until five years later, but when he returned to the dugout it was in the Bronx ... where he promptly won *five consecutive* World Series Titles on his way to seven total.

Roger McDowell

7 The 2012 season will be Roger McDowell's (7th) as pitching coach for the Braves. McDowell had a task that was almost as hard as following Bobby Cox as manager ... he had to follow Leo Mazzone as pitching coach. No worries, he was more than up for the challenge. The pitching staff has thrived, especially since 2009 when the club's starters had the lowest earned run average in baseball. And under his tutelage, youngsters like Tommy Hanson, Jair Jurrjens, and Jonny Venters have developed into stars.

Pat Corrales

9 After managing three teams and nine seasons, Pat Corrales joined the Braves staff and spent (9) successful seasons as the bench coach for Bobby Cox. Corrales has had an amazing 50-plus years in professional baseball and in his time with the Braves he was a great influence on many players—but he's often remembered for two incidents he'd probably rather forget, both occurring before his time in Atlanta. The first was a mound altercation with opposing pitcher Dave Stewart, who Corrales thought should have been ejected after throwing at Julio Franco. Corrales, who was managing the A's, began to exchange shouts with Stewart, and next thing you know Corrales charged the mound and kicked Stewart ... unfortunately, Stewart was big into martial arts, and he promptly decked Corrales, igniting a five-minute brawl and earning Corrales the moniker "KO Corrales" from ESPN's Chris Berman. "It wasn't a smart move," Corrales said later. The second incident was with the Phillies in 1983, when he became the first—and so far only—manager to be fired with his team in first place.

Bobby Cox

10 Only (10) managers in franchise history have led the club for five or more seasons—and only two of them managed five seasons in Atlanta. The first was Lum Harris, who led the Braves from 1968-72. And the second was, obviously, Bobby Cox, who managed 25 of the club's first 46 seasons in Atlanta.

Harry Wright

10 The Braves have also been managed by (10) Hall of Famers, including Harry Wright, who was the club's first manager in 1876. Of course most went into the Hall as players, but not Wright—he was inducted as a Pioneer / Executive in 1953 for his managerial skills and his role in developing the sport of professional baseball. Wright is credited as the first manager in history to win four consecutive Pennants, leading the National Association's Boston Red Stockings to consecutive titles from 1872-75, and for good measure he won two more in 1877-78 after the Red Stockings had joined the National League. Wright was a player-manager for five of his six Pennant-winning teams.

Glenn Hubbard

12 After ten seasons playing second base in Atlanta, Glenn Hubbard spent another (12) seasons coaching first base for the Braves from 1999-2010. Hubbard spent nine years coaching in the minors for the Braves, and among his many successes as a coach, it was Hubbard who successfully converted Kelly Johnson from an outfielder to a second baseman in preparation for the 2007 season.

Eddie Perez

18 Eddie Perez spent (18) of his 20 professional seasons playing in the Braves organization—including nine seasons in the big leagues—before he joined the coaching staff in 2007. Perez won MVP honors during the 1999 NLCS for the Braves and he also retired with a .464 career average in NLCS play, the highest in history for a catcher. The 2012 season will be his sixth as the Braves' bullpen coach.

Clarence Jones

38 The number of league leading home runs (38) for Clarence Jones in 1974. Mike Schmidt won his first home run title that season, hitting 36 for the Phillies, and Dick Allen won his second home run title in three seasons, hitting 32 for the White Sox. So ... who did Jones win his title with? Well, the Kintetsu Buffaloes of the Japanese Pacific League, of course. Jones only hit two home runs during 58 big league games in 1967-68, and that was the extent of his Major League career—but he was a hit in Japan. In 1974 he was the first foreigner to win a home run title in Japan, and he backed it up by leading the league again with 36 home runs two seasons later. Of course, Braves fans know him as the hitting coach who geared up the offense for the team's dominant 1990s teams. David Justice said of Jones, "He made a big impact on me ... he keeps me on track."

Fredi Gonzalez

47 Fredi Gonzalez became the (47th) manager in franchise history when he took the reigns in 2011. Gonzalez began his Braves' coaching career with Richmond in 2002, and in 2003 he joined the big club and coached third base for four years under Bobby Cox. His first managerial job in the majors was with the Florida Marlins. Gonzalez was 276-279 in Miami but the club fired him after 70 games in 2010. Almost immediately there was speculation that Gonzalez would replace Bobby Cox in Atlanta. His history and relationship with the team, with Bobby, and with the players was just too good to pass up. Frank Wren, who didn't even interview other candidates, said, "This is perfect for us on so many levels ... he was on our radar before he was available. We thought there may come a time when we were going to have to ask the Florida Marlins for permission to talk to their manager. We really thought Fredi was the best candidate for us." As for Gonzalez, when asked about replacing Bobby Cox, he said, "Our goal is simple: we want to keep putting flags on that façade up there. I don't think there's a person alive that's going to replace Bobby Cox—we just want to continue the winning tradition and go from there."

Bobby Dews

50 Bobby Dews played basketball and baseball for Georgia Tech and later he played and managed in the minors for the Cardinals organization. He began his coaching career with the Braves in 1974, and retired as the bullpen coach after 2006—but that didn't stop him from working. He continued working in a variety of roles with the club and in 2008 he began his 35th consecutive season with the Braves organization—and then in 2009, he marked his overall (50th) Major League Spring Training.

Bruce Dal Canton

51 The number of career wins (51) for Bruce Dal Canton during 11 seasons pitching in the big leagues. His story proves that hard work and tenacity improve both your luck and your talent. A former schoolteacher, DC was signed by the Pirates in 1966 as an amateur free agent after attending a Major League tryout camp. His career included a brief stop in Atlanta from 1975-76, but he really made his mark on the game as a highly respected coach. DC was the Braves pitching coach from 1987-90, and beginning in 1991 he began a long tenure as a minor league instructor for the club.

Lum Harris

93 Lum Harris managed the Braves to (93) wins in 1969 and the first Division Title in franchise history. Atlanta was in fifth place in late August, but after posting a 20-6 record in September—including a season best ten-game winning streak—the Braves overtook both the Giants and the Reds to claim the Division.

Terry Pendleton

339 The Braves (.339) team on-base percentage led the National League in 2010 during Terry Pendleton's ninth and final season as hitting coach. It was yet another successful year for Pendleton, but with the hiring of Fredi Gonzalez, he made the move to first base coach in 2011. Among his many successes during his tenure as the Braves hitting coach, Pendleton changed Andruw Jones' approach at the plate in 2005—and then Jones hit a team record 51 home runs. Under Pendleton's leadership, the Braves also led the league in home runs in 2006, set a franchise record for doubles in 2007, and then in 2008, Chipper Jones won the Braves' first batting titles since— ironically—Terry Pendleton, in 1991.

Rogers Hornsby

387 The batting average (.387) for player-manager Rogers Hornsby in 1928. That'd be even more impressive if not for the fact it was .057 points higher than the team's winning percentage … in his only year with the Braves, the Hall of Fame legend posted unbelievable numbers offensively, but he had no luck whatsoever with the only stat that matters: winning. The club began the season 11-20, and then Hornsby took over managerial duties from Jack Slattery. It didn't matter. The Braves were just 39-83 under Hornsby, and 50-103 overall. The next season Hornsby was league MVP for the Pennant-winning Cubs.

George Stallings

492 The winning percentage (.492) for George Stallings during eight seasons managing the Braves from 1913-20. Stallings only had three winning seasons with the Braves, but as it happens, one of those seasons was 1914—the "Miracle Braves" team that won the first World Series Title in franchise history.

Joe Torre

529 The winning percentage (.529) for Joe Torre during three seasons managing the club from 1982-84. The last time the Braves went to the postseason without Bobby Cox as manager, the man leading the club was Joe Torre. Ironically, Torre took over managerial duties *from* Cox in 1982, and then led the club to its first Division Title since 1969. It was Torre's first taste of the postseason—he'd somehow played 2,209 Major League games in 18 seasons without making it to the postseason—and it ended in disappointment, as the

Braves were swept by the Cardinals in the League Championship Series.

Billy Southworth

542 The winning percentage (.542) for Hall of Fame manager Billy Southworth during six seasons leading the Boston Braves from 1946-51. After 1914, the Braves didn't win another Pennant until 1948, when Southworth, who'd won two World Series Titles managing the Cardinals, guided the club to a league best 91-62 record.

Fred Haney

596 The winning percentage (.596) for Fred Haney during four seasons managing the Milwaukee Braves from 1956-59. For modern era managers with at least four years leading the club, that's the highest winning percentage in franchise history. Haney took over managerial duties in mid-1956 and led the club to a 68-40 record the rest of the way—an impressive .630 winning percentage. His success continued in his first full season at the helm, as Haney guided the Braves to the second World Championship in franchise history in a thrilling seven-game series vs. the New York Yankees. In 1958, Haney became the first Braves' manager in the modern era to lead the team to back-to-back Pennants. Bobby Cox managed the Braves during 15 of the first 21 postseasons in franchise history—and of the six managers who've guided the club to the postseason, only Cox and Haney did so more than once.

Frank Selee

607 The winning percentage (.607) for Hall of Fame manager Frank Selee during 12 seasons leading the Boston Beaneaters. Vern Benson is the only undefeated manager in franchise history … having earned that distinction by virtue of winning his only game at the helm in 1977, something Ted Turner was unable to do that same season. Among managers with more experience than a single game, Jim Hart was 83-45 during 133 games in 1889, good for a .648 winning percentage that's the highest in franchise history. Among managers with more than one year guiding the club, however, no one was better than Frank Selee. He won 1,004 games in 12 seasons, and lost only 649. He won six Pennants, and had just one losing season—and that wasn't until his second to last as skipper.

Greg Walker

1,791 The number of home runs (1,791) hit by the Chicago White Sox from 2003-11. The third highest total in the majors during that time, they came during Greg Walker's tenure as hitting coach. The White Sox also boasted the majors seventh best slugging percentage in that span. Walker is a Georgia native, and after the offense struggled in 2011 the Braves decided to bring him on board as the new hitting coach. Frank Wren said, "We wanted someone who had recent Major League experience in this role and that had a reputation for understanding the swing and an ability to communicate … Greg epitomized all three." After the front office announced his hiring, Walker said, "It's pretty humbling that the team you grew up with trusts you to do a real important job for them."

Chuck Tanner

2,738 Chuck Tanner won (2,738) games as a big league manager. He also managed the Pittsburgh Pirates to a World Championship in 1979. He was less successful with the Braves, however—winning just 153 games and losing 208. Tanner actually made a bit of history in his Major League debut as a player, for the Milwaukee Braves, no less. On April 12, 1955, with the Braves down 2-1 vs. Cincinnati in the eighth inning, Tanner pinch-hit for Hall of Fame legend Warren Spahn. It was the first at bat of his career, and on the very first pitch he hit a game-tying home run. He hit only 21 in his career, but he was the first player in Major League history to hit a pinch-hit home run in his first big league at bat.

*"Greg Maddux could put a baseball through
a lifesaver if you asked him."*
— Joe Morgan

7 CY YOUNG WORTHY

THE ATLANTA BRAVES dominant run in the 1990s was fueled by a pitching staff that achieved unprecedented success. A glance at the Cy Young voting from 1991-2000 illustrates this perfectly.

1991 – Glavine (1st), Avery (6th)
1992 – Glavine (2nd)
1993 – Maddux (1st), Glavine (3rd)
1994 – Maddux (1st)
1995 – Maddux (1st), Glavine (3rd)
1996 – Smoltz (1st), Maddux (5th)
1997 – Maddux (2nd), Neagle (3rd)
1998 – Glavine (1st), Maddux (4th), Smoltz (4th)
1999 – Millwood (3rd)
2000 – Glavine (2nd), Maddux (3rd)

The Cy Young was awarded to a Braves' pitcher six times— the most won by any team in a single decade in history. For ten consecutive years the Braves had at least one pitcher place in the top three in Cy Young balloting, six times in that span the Braves had at least two pitchers in the top five—and in three of the four seasons that a member of the Braves' staff didn't win the Cy Young, either

Glavine or Maddux placed second in balloting. In this chapter we take a look back at the Braves' Cy Young recipients and other great seasons that were Cy Young worthy.

Warren Spahn

6 Warren Spahn's remarkable run of (6) consecutive 20-win seasons began in 1956. He was 20-11 with a 2.78 earned run average, but oddly enough, it was one of the few seasons in his career that he did not lead the league in any major category. Despite that, his numbers were still good enough that he placed third in Major League Cy Young balloting.

Greg Maddux & Denny Neagle

9 Greg Maddux and Denny Neagle combined to make 67 starts for the Braves in 1997—and total, they suffered just (9) losses. Maddux (19-4) led the league with a .826 winning percentage and Neagle (20-5) led the league in wins, but Pedro Martinez (17-8, 1.90 earned run average for the Expos) won the Cy Young Award with Maddux (2nd) and Neagle (3rd) rounding out the top three. Neagle was the fourth different Braves' pitcher to lead the league in wins during the 1990s—and in fact, the only season from 1991-2000 that a member of the Braves' staff did not lead the league in wins was 1999, when Mike Hampton won a league best 22 games for the Astros (Maddux was third that season with 19).

Tom Glavine

9 The number of complete games (9) for Tom Glavine during his 1991 Cy Young season. That total led the league and established a career high for Glavine. He also won 20 games for the first time, tying for the league lead. Glavine was a 20-game winner five times from 1991-2000, and he led the league each time.

Tom Glavine

13 Tom Glavine led the league in wins for the second consecutive season in 1992, including (13) in a row from May 27 – August 19, which was a record at that time. Glavine was 9-0 in July and August. He was 20-8 overall with a 2.76 earned run average, and he also led the league with a career high five shutouts. Glavine followed his 1991 Cy Young campaign with some very impressive numbers—including just six home runs allowed in 225 innings—but he missed out on back-to-back Cy Young Awards when he placed second in balloting to the Cubs' Greg Maddux.

Phil Niekro

18 Phil Niekro led the league with (18) complete games in 1974. He also led the league in wins and innings pitched, with 302 innings and a 20-13 record. It was the second career 20-win season for Niekro, and the first time he led the league in wins. He also posted an impressive 2.38 earned run average, but placed a disappointing third in Cy Young balloting.

Warren Spahn

18 Vern Law and Warren Spahn tied for the league lead with (18) complete games in 1960. Law was 20-9 for the Pirates—the only 20-win season of his career—and Spahn was a league best 21-10 for the Braves. Law had 120 strikeouts, Spahn had 154. Law had three shutouts, Spahn had four. The only significant stat where Law really had an edge was ERA—Law's was 3.08, Spahn's was 3.50. It was Law, however, who won Cy Young honors, with Spahn placing second.

Warren Spahn

18 The number of complete games (18) for Warren Spahn during his 1957 Cy Young season. It was the third time he led the league in complete games, but it was also the beginning of a remarkable stretch for the 36-year-old veteran ... Spahn led the league in complete games seven consecutive seasons from 1957-63. He also led the league with 21 wins in 1957, and that began a five-year run from 1957-61 in which he also led the league in wins every season.

Warren Spahn

21 Warren Spahn won (21) games in 1961. It was his sixth consecutive 20-win season, and his fifth consecutive season leading the league in wins. Spahn also led the league with a 3.02 earned run average, and the 40-year-old lefty placed second in Cy Young balloting for the third time in four seasons.

Russ Ortiz

21 Atlanta traded lefty Damian Moss to San Francisco to acquire Russ Ortiz, who had won 18, 14, 17, and 14 games during four full seasons with the Giants. Ortiz exceeded all expectations under the guidance of Leo Mazzone, setting a career high and leading the league with (21) victories—and for his efforts he placed fourth in Cy Young balloting. Dodgers' closer Eric Gagne won the award that season on the strength of 55 saves. Jason Schmidt (17-5) was the runner-up and Mark Prior (18-6) placed third. Ortiz's chances at winning the Cy Young were hurt significantly by his 3.81 earned run average—despite the fact he was the league's only 20-game winner, he also gave up nearly 1.50 more earned runs per game than Schmidt or Prior.

Tom Glavine

22 Tom Glavine won a career high (22) games in 1993. It was the third consecutive season he led the league in wins, but he only placed third in Cy Young balloting behind teammate Greg Maddux and Cardinals' closer Lee Smith. Glavine was an astounding 13-3 after July 1, as the Braves and Giants battled it out for the NL West Title.

Phil Niekro

23 Phil Niekro won a career high (23) games in 1969. He was 23-13 with a 2.56 earned run average, and he placed second in Cy Young balloting. That's as close as he ever got to being named the league's top pitcher, despite 318 career wins.

Tom Glavine

28 Tom Glavine was 16-7 with a 3.08 earned run average during the 1995 regular season—numbers that placed him third in Cy Young balloting behind teammate Greg Maddux and Cincinnati's Pete Schourek. It was the fourth time in five seasons that Glavine placed third or higher in Cy Young balloting, but as good as his numbers were that season, it's what Glavine did during the postseason that fans remember. In four starts and (28) innings of work, he gave up just 16 hits and five earned runs. His most memorable start, of course, was Game 6 of the World Series when he tossed eight shutout innings and gave up just one hit in the Title-clenching victory vs. Cleveland.

Tom Glavine & Greg Maddux

40 Tom Glavine and Greg Maddux combined to win (40) games for the Braves in 2000. Glavine was 21-9 and led the league in wins. Maddux was 19-9 and third in the league in wins. Arizona's Randy Johnson (19 wins, 347 strikeouts) won his second consecutive Cy Young Award, but for the fourth and final time as teammates, Glavine (2nd) and Maddux (3rd) both finished in the top four in Cy Young balloting during the same season.

Warren Spahn & Lew Burdette

42 Warren Spahn and Lew Burdette combined to win (42) games as the Braves won a second consecutive Pennant in 1958. Spahn led the league with 22 wins and Burdette, who was third in the league with 20 wins, led the league with a .667 winning percentage. Bob Turley, who was 21-7 for the Yankees, won the Cy Young Award by a single vote. Spahn was second in the balloting, Burdette was third, and unfortunately, the Yankees beat the Braves in the World Series as well.

John Smoltz

55 John Smoltz set a National League record with (55) saves in 2002. A year later, Gagne would win the Cy Young after tying Smoltz's record, however, Smoltz was only third in the 2002 balloting—one place ahead of Gagne, who saved 52 games for the Dodgers. Randy Johnson won the 2002 NL Cy Young Award after posting a 24-5 record with 334 strikeouts for the Diamondbacks. Curt Schilling, Johnson's teammate, placed second in the balloting with a 23-7 record and 316 strikeouts. For Smoltz, it was his highest finish in Cy Young balloting during his years closing for the Braves.

Greg Maddux & John Smoltz

60 Greg Maddux and John Smoltz combined to start (60) games for the Braves in 1998. Atlanta won 41 times when Maddux or Smoltz started—including a 22-4 record during 26 starts for Smoltz. Eight of the 15 games the Braves lost when Maddux started were by a single run, and in three of the losses the Braves offense was shut out completely. Tom Glavine won his second Cy Young after he posted the league's best record at 20-6, and his teammates Maddux (18-9, league best 2.22 earned run average) and Smoltz (17-3, league best .850 winning percentage) tied for fourth in the balloting. Glavine, Maddux, and Smoltz dominated the Cy Young voting during the 1990s, but 1998 was the only season in which all three placed in the top five in balloting.

Greg Maddux

156 The league leading earned run average (1.56) for Greg Maddux during his 1994 Cy Young season. In only 25 starts, Maddux was 16-6 with ten complete games and a ridiculous .896 ratio of walks plus hits per innings pitched (WHIP). He was the unanimous choice for his third consecutive Cy Young, and his second in two seasons with the Braves. As great as his stats were that season, what he did during 13 starts on the road was even more impressive—Maddux was 10-2 with a 1.37 ERA, four complete games, and only 79 hits allowed in 105 innings pitched.

Greg Maddux

267 The league high number of innings (267) pitched by Greg Maddux during his 1993 Cy Young season. People remember how nasty his stuff was, but they often forget he was also a workhorse on the mound. It was the third of five consecutive seasons from 1991-95 that he led the league in innings pitched. Mad Dog also led the league with eight complete games—and he led the league again in 1994, and yet again in 1995. There are some great quotes by Maddux's peers about how dominant he was during the four consecutive seasons he won the National League Cy Young Award from 1992-95. One of the best is by Dwight Gooden, who said, "He makes it look easy. You wish there was another league he could get called up to."

John Smoltz

276 John Smoltz led the league with a career high (276) strikeouts during his 1996 Cy Young season. Smoltz was 24-8, which gave him six more wins than the next highest total in the league. In fact, when

Smoltz tied for the league lead in wins a decade later his total was only 16 ... eight *fewer* than his 1996 total, but still the highest in the league. Smoltz was able to win so many games in 1996 because he got off to a scorching start and then stayed consistent the entire season. He was the National League Pitcher of the Month in April and May, after he was 5-1 and 6-0 in the season's first two months. He had at least 45 strikeouts in every month except July, when he had one less start due to the All-Star break, and he was 3-2, 3-2, 3-2, and 4-1 over the final four months of the season.

Tim Hudson

283 The earned run average (2.83) for Tim Hudson in 2010. A year removed from successful Tommy John surgery, Hudson was 17-9 with the league's sixth best ERA—and as a result he earned the 2010 National league Comeback Player of the Year Award and placed fourth in Cy Young balloting. In August, as the Braves were battling to make the playoffs in Bobby Cox's final season, Hudson was at his absolute best. He was 4-0 with a 1.71 ERA during six starts. Hudson had back-to-back starts in which he pitched eight scoreless innings, and he pitched deep into his other four starts as well, and gave up more than two runs only once.

Steve Avery

692 The winning percentage (.692) for 21-year-old lefty Steve Avery in 1991. He was 18-8 with a 3.38 earned run average during his second big league season. Avery's win total was third highest in the league, and earned him a sixth place showing in Cy Young balloting.

Phil Niekro

810 Hall of Fame legend Phil Niekro had Cy Young worthy seasons in three different decades with the Braves. In 1982, the 43-year-old knuckleballer led the league with a (.810) winning percentage. He was 17-4 with a 3.61 earned run average, but he only placed fifth in Cy Young balloting.

Tom Glavine

857 The winning percentage (.857) for Tom Glavine during 17 road starts in his 1998 Cy Young season. Glavine won the award for the second time after posting a league best 20-6 overall record, and he was an astounding 12-2 on the road. The record is impressive, but the really crazy stat is his earned run average on the road was more than 1.50 points below his earned run average at home. Glavine was fourth in the league with a 2.47 ERA overall—but his road ERA was only 1.78, as opposed to his 3.32 ERA at home.

Greg Maddux

905 Greg Maddux set a franchise record with his (.905) winning percentage during his 1995 Cy Young season. In 28 starts, Maddux was 19-2 with a 1.63 earned run average. He led the league in wins, winning percentage, ERA, complete games (10), shutouts (3), innings pitched (209), and WHIP (.811, also a franchise record and the sixth best in Major League history). He was the unanimous Cy Young winner again, and also for the second consecutive season what he did on the road was insane. In 15 road starts, Maddux was 13-0 with a 1.12 ERA. He gave up only 70 hits and 11 walks in 112 innings ... that's a .719 WHIP.

Kevin Millwood

996 Kevin Millwood's (0.996) walks plus hits per inning ratio led the league in 1999. Millwood was second on the Braves' staff with 18 wins and his .720 winning percentage was the best among Braves' starters. The 24-year-old right-hander, in just his second full season with the club, made 33 starts and posted a career best 2.68 earned run average. He gave up only 168 hits and 61 walks, but pitched 228 innings. For his efforts, Millwood placed third in Cy Young balloting behind Randy Johnson (Diamondbacks) and Mike Hampton (Astros). It was the first time since 1990 that Tom Glavine, John Smoltz, or Greg Maddux did not finish among the top three in Cy Young Balloting—but Millwood kept the Braves' streak alive, giving the club at least one pitcher in the top three every season from 1991-2000.

"He told us how proud he was. I really think out of all the teams, he's got a soft spot in his heart for this club right here. This club went above and beyond what was expected once the injury bug hit."
— Chipper Jones, when asked what Bobby Cox said to the team after the Giants eliminated the Braves in the 2010 postseason

8 THE TEAMS

THE BRAVES ARE the oldest, continuously operating professional sports franchise in America. It began as the Boston Red Stockings in the 1870s and continues today as the only franchise to field a team in every season that professional baseball has been played. The Red Stockings played in the first ever National League game on April 22, 1876, and they won six of the first eight Pennants in baseball history—four in the National Association and two in the National League. There were many name changes—first the Beaneaters, later the Doves and the Rustlers, and finally in 1912, for the first time, the Braves. The 1914 "Miracle Braves" won the first modern era World Championship in franchise history and remain one of the most loved and best-known teams in baseball history.

The Braves became the Bees in 1936, changed back to the Braves in 1940, but by the 1950s it was clear the team was ready for a move. The fan base in Boston was behind the Red Sox, so the Braves moved to Milwaukee—after 82 years in Boston—in time for the 1953 season. Lack of support in Milwaukee brought the Braves to Atlanta in 1966. Cable TV brought the Braves into homes all across America in the 1970s, by the 1980s the Braves were "America's Team," and by the 1990s the Braves were the most dominant team in baseball. What follows is a look at some of the most successful teams in franchise history, by the numbers.

1914

614 The winning percentage (.614) during the regular season for the 1914 "Miracle Braves." The club started the season just 4-18, and was dead last, 11 games out of first, on July 18. However, after a torrid 51-16 finish, the Braves finished the season 94-59 and won the Pennant by an astounding 10.5 games over the Giants. Bill James, Dick Rudolph, and Lefty Tyler then led the Braves to a shocking sweep over the favored Philadelphia Athletics in the World Series, surrendering just five earned runs in the series.

1948

338 The Braves' pitching staff led the league with a (3.38) earned run average in 1948. Johnny Sain emerged as the team's top pitcher with a 24-15 record and 2.60 ERA—and this is the season when the phrase "Spahn and Sain and two days of rain" was coined. The Braves also batted .275 as a team, best in the league. That combination of pitching and offense led to 91 wins and the second Pennant in team history. One of the best postseason games in franchise history came during the 1948 World Series vs. Cleveland. In Game 1, Johnny Sain outdueled Hall of Famer Bob Feller, 1-0. The two teams combined for just six hits, and the Braves had only two, but managed to push across the game's only run in the eighth inning when Tommy Holmes singled home Phil Masi with two outs. It was a hard-fought series, but Cleveland would go on to win in six games.

1953

1,826,297 The Braves began play in Milwaukee in 1953 and set a league record for attendance as (1,826,297) fans came out to Milwaukee County Stadium. There was plenty to cheer for, as well— Eddie Mathews hit 47 home runs and Warren Spahn won 23 games, both were best in the league. The Braves won 92 games and were in first place until an eight-game losing streak in late June derailed what had been a solid start to the season. The Braves recovered in August, winning 23 times in 32 games, but by then the Dodgers had steamrolled the rest of the league. Brooklyn ended up winning the Pennant by 13 games over the second place Braves.

1956

12 The Braves beat the Dodgers (12) times in 1956, losing just ten of the 22 meetings between the two rivals. And yet, despite being in first place 110 days throughout the season, having never trailed by more than 3.5 games at any point during the season, and having led by 3.5 games on September 3, the Braves suffered a season high five-game losing streak in early September and then split two games with the Dodgers the following week … which gave the Dodgers a one-game lead with less than three weeks left on the schedule. The two teams battled it out over the final 18 days of the season, ending six of those days tied at the top of the standings. But on September 29, the second to last day of the season, the Braves began play with a half-game lead, only to lose 2-1 to St. Louis. The Dodgers swept a doubleheader at home vs. Pittsburgh, and suddenly the Braves were a game back with one left to play. Milwaukee beat St. Louis 4-2 in the must-win season finale, but the Dodgers also won, beating Pittsburgh 8-6 and eliminating the Braves on the season's final day.

1957

818 The winning percentage (.818) for the Braves during 22 games vs. Cincinnati in 1957. The Braves were 18-4 vs. the Reds, including a three-game sweep from August 6 – 8. The Braves began that series trailing the Cardinals by one game in the NL Pennant race, but after the sweep the club had not only regained the lead but also found itself in the midst of a season high ten-game winning streak. In that streak, the Braves beat the Reds six times—three at home, three on the road, and went from one game back in the standings to *eight games ahead* in only 12 days. The 1957 Braves could do little wrong—Hank Aaron won MVP honors, Warren Spahn won the Cy Young, and the club won the Pennant by eight games over the Cardinals. Aaron then batted .393 in the World Series, Lew Burdette won three games, and the Braves beat the Yankees in seven games for the second World Championship in franchise history.

1958

266 The defending World Champion Braves boasted a powerful lineup that batted (.266) in 1958—the highest team average in the league. Led by Hank Aaron (.326, 30 HR), Eddie Mathews (.251, 31 HR), Wes Covington (.330, 24 HR), Joe Adcock (.275, 19 HR), and Del Crandall (.272, 18 HR) the Braves were also fourth in the league in scoring, hits, and home runs. Along with a potent offense, the Braves had a starting rotation that included Warren Spahn and Lew Burdette, who combined for 42 wins. All total the club won 92 games and a second consecutive Pennant before falling to the Yankees in a tough seven-game World Series.

1959

86 The Braves spent (86) days in first place in 1959. Trying for a third consecutive Pennant, the Braves were again locked in a duel down the stretch with the Dodgers. And again, the season would end in disappointment. The Braves and the Dodgers began play tied for first place on the season's final day, and both teams won—forcing a best-of-three series to determine the league champion. The Braves fell at home 3-2 in the opener, and then lost in LA 6-5. The Dodgers went on to beat the White Sox in the World Series.

1963

677 The Braves scored (677) runs in 1963. With 84 wins, the Braves were well back in the standings and finished in sixth place. However, two of the biggest names in baseball history had extraordinary individual accomplishments for the Braves that season. Led by slugger Hank Aaron, the offense was actually in fine form. The Braves were second in home runs and third in runs as Bad Henry made a run at the Triple Crown. He led the league with 44 home runs and 130 RBIs, and for good measure he also led the league with 121 runs, but his .319 average was third best in the league, just .007 points behind the Dodgers' Tommy Davis. The Braves' pitching staff was middle of the pack in 1963, but 42-year-old Warren Spahn led the club with a 23-7 record and 2.60 earned run average. Leave it to the Dodgers to keep getting in the way ... Sandy Koufax (25-5) won the MVP Award and the Cy Young Award in 1963.

1966

13 The franchise officially became the Atlanta Braves on April 12, 1966, and the Braves first game in Atlanta lasted (13) innings. It was a 3-2 loss vs. Pittsburgh, with Willie Stargell hitting a two-run shot for the Pirates in the top of the thirteenth. Joe Torre was the first Braves' player to homer in Atlanta, hitting two solo shots for the only offense of the night for the Braves. Tony Cloninger also went into the record book, as he received the team's first loss. The Braves lost again the next night, 6-0, and then they hit the road. Atlanta won four of six on the trip and then returned home to face the Mets on April 22. Cloninger got into the record book again, on a good note this time. He was the winning pitcher in the Braves 8-4 victory over the Mets—the first home win for the Atlanta Braves. The inaugural Atlanta Braves team won 85 games and finished fifth in the league standings. Team leaders included Hank Aaron with 44 home runs and 127 RBIs, Joe Torre with a .315 average, 36 home runs, and 101 RBIs, and Felipe Alou with a .327 average and 36 home runs. Tony Cloninger and Ken Johnson tied for the team lead with 14 wins each.

1968

2.92 The Braves set an Atlanta-era record with a (2.92) team earned run average in 1968. Pitching was dominating baseball at the time, as evidenced by this fact: despite setting a team record, the staff ERA was only *sixth best* in the league. The 1968 Braves also set a franchise record on offense … unfortunately, it wasn't good. The team scored just 514 runs, the lowest total in team history, and the result was a fifth place finish at 81-81.

1969

93 Just one year later though, the Braves won (93) games and the first NL West Division Title in league history. The offense was much improved, scoring 691 runs and ranking third in the league in both average and home runs, and the Braves battled the Giants and Reds all season, never trailing by more than three games and never leading by more than four. The Braves had the strongest finish to the season, winning 20 of 27 games down the stretch to claim the Title by three games over the Giants. The Braves faced the Mets in the very first National League Championship Series, with the Mets sweeping the best-of-five series.

1991

165 As the Braves went from "Worst-to-First" the offense set an Atlanta-era record by stealing (165) bases. The Braves speed on the base paths contributed to the offense scoring the second highest runs total in the league. Otis Nixon led the way with 72 steals, followed by Ron Gant with 34.

1992

24 The Braves set a franchise record with (24) shutouts in 1992. With 98 wins on the season, that means nearly 1 in 4 victories was a shutout. Pretty incredible. The 1992 Braves also set franchise records with three consecutive shutouts and 36 consecutive scoreless innings. The staff led the league with a 3.14 earned run average, and unlike the 1968 club, the Braves offense was the third highest scoring in the league—all of which added up to a second consecutive Pennant.

1993

740 The Braves winning percentage (.740) after the 1993 All-Star break. Atlanta was 54-19, the third best second half surge in Major League history. The Braves faced a ten-game deficit in late July, but it was completely erased with a 3-2 victory in San Diego on September 10. The Braves won on the season's final day, the Giants lost, and Atlanta became the first team to win three consecutive NL West Titles. For the first time since 1970 (Aaron, Cepeda, and Carty), the Braves boasted three players with 100-plus RBIs (McGriff, Justice, and Gant). The 1993 team was also the first to lead the NL in both home runs (168) and earned run average (3.14) in consecutive seasons since the 1977-78 Dodgers. There's more: the Braves starting rotation boasted four 15-game winners for the first time in franchise history (Maddux, Glavine, Avery, and Smoltz)—and Tom Glavine became the first NL pitcher with three consecutive 20-win seasons since Hall of Famer Fergie Jenkins in 1967-69.

1995

540 The Braves' pitching staff gave up just (540) runs during the 1995 regular season. The lowest total in the league, only 494 of those runs were earned for a league best 3.44 earned run average. The Braves' pitching staff continued to find success in the 1995 postseason. Atlanta won the best-of-five Division Series in four games over the Rockies, the best-of-seven League Championship Series in four games over the Reds, and the World Series in six games over the Indians. The Braves became the first franchise in baseball history to win the World Series three times for three different cities (Boston, Milwaukee, and Atlanta).

1996

56 In the final season at Atlanta-Fulton County Stadium the Braves set a franchise record with (56) home wins. It was a fitting send off for the stadium, as the Braves had yet another extraordinary season. Atlanta won its fifth consecutive Division Title, claiming the NL East by eight games and becoming the first NL team in history to win five consecutive Division crowns. The offense was powerful, hitting 197 home runs—at the time, the third highest total in franchise history. The pitching was overpowering—striking out a Major League record 1,245 batters while issuing the fewest walks in baseball. John Smoltz won the Cy Young and set a franchise record for strikeouts. Mark Wohlers set a franchise record with 39 saves. And the list goes on ... Andruw Jones made his debut, belted two home runs in the World Series ... Jermaine Dye homered in his first big league at bat ... Marquis Grissom had 207 hits, a 28-game hitting streak, and a straight steal of home ... about the only thing that didn't go right for the Braves was losing the World Series after winning the first two games of the series in New York. And yet ... the Braves were named *Baseball America* Organization of the Year for 1996.

1997

12 The Braves' offense set a team record with (12) grand slams in 1997. Chipper Jones led the way with a team record three grand slams in a span of just 13 games, and overall the club was second in the league in homers and third in the league in scoring. Combine that with a pitching staff that led the league with a 3.18 earned run average and you get 101 wins. Unfortunately, 1997 was the year the Marlins won the Wild Card and surprised everyone in baseball by beating the Braves in the NLCS and the Indians in the World Series.

1998

106 The 1998 Braves won a franchise record (106) games. The club scored 826 runs, but gave up just 581—and won the Division by 18 games over the Mets, 31 games over the Phillies, 41 games over the Expos, and 52 games over the Marlins. After beating the Cubs in the Division Series, the Braves advanced to the League Championship Series for the seventh consecutive postseason.

1999

8 The 1999 Braves appeared in a record (8th) consecutive League Championship Series. Chipper Jones singlehandedly disposed of the Mets during his MVP season, blowing open what for a time was a tight race for the NL East. Atlanta cruised to the Division Title with 103 wins, only to faceoff against the Wild Card Mets in the League Championship Series. After Atlanta won the first three games of the series, the Mets won Games 4 and 5 to make things interesting ... but the Braves claimed the Pennant in Game 6 and advanced to the World Series for the fifth time in the 1990s. Unfortunately, the Yankees swept the series.

2000

95 The 2000 Braves won (95) games and a ninth consecutive Division Title. The Braves became just the third team in baseball history to win 90-plus games in consecutive completed seasons (discounting the strike-shortened 1994 season), joining the Yankees and Cubs. Atlanta won 15 consecutive games this year, setting a franchise record. Chipper Jones had 111 RBIs and became just the second third baseman in baseball history with five consecutive seasons of 100-plus RBIs. And the pitching staff … well, it wasn't as good as years past. The team earned run average slipped up to 4.06, the highest since 1990, and yet … it was *still* the best in baseball for the fourth consecutive season and for the seventh time in nine seasons overall. Greg Maddux won 19 games, making him just the third player in history to win 15-plus games in 13 consecutive seasons. Unfortunately, the streak of eight consecutive appearances in the NLCS ended as the Cardinals swept the Braves in the Division Series.

2001

88 Atlanta made its tenth consecutive postseason despite winning just (88) games during the regular season. That's the fewest wins by a Braves team to make the postseason during baseball's modern era. In fact, only twice in that time has a Braves team failed to make the playoffs after winning 90-plus games during the regular season: in 1953, and again in 1956. Both times the Braves placed second in the Pennant race—the other 19 times that the Braves won 90 or more games, the club made the playoffs. So of course, in 2011 the Braves won 89 games …

2002

808 The winning percentage (.808) for the Braves in June 2002. Atlanta was 4.5 games back of the Mets and Expos on May 1, but overcame that deficit to grab a half-game lead by the end of the month. What the Braves did in June, however, was just ridiculous. Atlanta was 21-5 and by July 1 its lead had soared to 9.5 games. The Braves cruised to yet another Division Title, clinching on September 9, the earliest in franchise history, and finishing 19 games ahead of the Expos, 21.5 ahead of Philly, 23 ahead of the Marlins, and 26.5

games in front of the last place Mets. The postseason ended in disappointment again, however—as Barry Bonds and the Giants beat the Braves in a tough five-game Division Series.

2003

907 The Braves scored (907) runs in 2003—a franchise record. No surprise, in 2003 the offense also set new marks with 1,608 hits, 321 doubles, 235 home runs, 587 extra-base hits, and 2,696 total bases. The pitching actually did have a subpar year this time—but the offense was best in the league, and the club won 101 games and another Division Title.

2004

2,000 The 2004 Braves gave Bobby Cox his (2,000th) career managerial win. Cox was just the ninth manager in history to achieve that milestone. And oh yeah, the Braves also won 96 games and another Division Title. John Smoltz saved 44 games and surpassed Gene Garber as the franchise leader for career saves with 154. The pitching staff led all of baseball in earned run average for the tenth time in 13 seasons … and that's with Smoltz in the bullpen, Maddux in Chicago, and Glavine in New York. Just how good was Leo Mazzone? Jaret Wright and Russ Ortiz led the 2004 rotation—*that's* how good Mazzone was.

2005

18 The Braves suffered so many injuries in 2005 that the club used (18) rookies to field lineups that season. Andruw Jones' 51 home runs was a big help, for sure, and John Smoltz returning to the rotation and winning 14 games was also huge as this team persevered and endured and fought its way to 90 wins and another Division Title. The 2005 Braves were the first team in baseball history to reach the postseason with five rookies who all had 100-plus at bats during the regular season: Wilson Betemit, Pete Orr, Kelly Johnson, Jeff Francoeur, and Brian McCann. No other team had made the postseason with more than four such rookies.

"The streak is one thing. I'm more disappointed in the loss. It was a fun run but all things have got to end sometime. I had fun with it. We had a nice little roll as a team and we're looking to get back on track tomorrow."
— *Dan Uggla, after his Atlanta record 33-game hitting streak ended*

9 FRANCHISE RECORDS

THE BRAVES FRANCHISE record books are filled with all the names you'd expect to find: Aaron, Mathews, Spahn, Niekro, Murphy, Jones, Maddux, Glavine, and Smoltz to name just a few ... but it's not limited to players who achieved superstar status wearing a Braves uniform. From the greatest games to the greatest seasons, the players who have performed at the highest possible level and achieved more than anyone before or since have been a mix of rookies and veterans, household names and one-year wonders, and franchise players and utility players.

In this chapter we look at 25 team records from the Atlanta-era of franchise history, by the numbers.

Tony Cloninger

2 On July 3, 1966, Tony Cloninger became the first player in National League history to hit (2) grand slams in the same game as the Braves beat the Giants 17-3. FYI, he was also the winning pitcher—and he tossed a complete game, no less. Cloninger's two grand slams and nine RBIs are both Atlanta records.

Charlie Leibrandt

3 Charlie Leibrandt was 15-7 for the Braves in 1992. And remarkably, he set an Atlanta record by winning (3) of those games by the score of 1-0. No other pitcher in Atlanta history has pitched as many 1-0 games in the course of one season.

Bob Horner

4 Bob Horner tied a Major League record when he hit (4) home runs vs. Montreal on July 6, 1986. He was 4 for 5, with six RBIs—and his slugging percentage shot up from .459 to .507. Horner, who hit only one home run in his next 28 games, later said, "The whole game, we're behind. Every time I came up to bat, we're behind, so the pitchers, luckily for me, are trying to come after me because they had nothing to lose. The stars aligned. They're throwing at me and trying to get me out and we're behind every time we're at bat. It happened, and my only regret is we didn't win." Only 15 players in history have had a four-homer game—three of them played for the Braves franchise. Bobby Lowe did it for the Beaneaters in 1894 and Joe Adcock did it for Milwaukee in 1954.

Chipper Jones

5 On August 30, 1997, Chipper Jones became the first player in

Atlanta history to score (5) runs in a single game. On July 3, 2001, he did it again.

Felix Millan

6 The Atlanta record for hits (6) in a single game. Three-time All-Star Felix Millan was the first player in Atlanta history to achieve this feat. On July 6, 1970, he was 6 for 6 with a double, triple, two runs, and four RBIs. On July 21, 2007, Willie Harris became the second player to have a 6 for 6 game for the Braves. Harris had four singles, two triples, four runs, six RBIs, and a stolen base. In total, seven players in franchise history have collected six hits in a game—but only two of them did so for Atlanta.

Otis Nixon

6 The Atlanta record for most steals in a game is also (6). Otis Nixon was 3 for 5 with two runs and six steals vs. Montreal on June 16, 1991. He singled, stole second, and stole third ... three different times. Nixon was the first player in National League history to record six steals in a single game—and he also set an Atlanta season record with 72 steals total in 1991.

Andres Galarraga

8 The Big Cat set an Atlanta record with (8) multi-home run games in 1998. He hit 44 bombs on the season, but the way he hit them was remarkable—he had a two-homer game in April, and then in June he had three two-homer games in a span of ten days, and four two-homer games for the month. He had a pair of two-homer games in July, and for good measure he had a two-homer game in August. Javy Lopez tied this record in 2003. Lopez had a two-homer game in April, a two-homer game in May, and then in June, Lopez had an astounding stretch in which he hit seven home runs in six games, including at least one home run in four consecutive games, and back-to-back two-homer games. Still in June, but ten days later … Lopez had another two-homer game, and two days later, another two-homer game. Ridiculous. He wasn't done. In late July, Lopez hit five home runs in five games—including another two-homer game. For good measure, Lopez added his eighth two-homer game of the season in August. Add them all up, he finished the season with a career high 43 bombs.

Andruw Jones

9 Andruw Jones had at least one RBI in (9) consecutive games from April 29 to May 8, 2003. That amazing streak established an Atlanta record. He had four home runs and 14 RBIs in that stretch.

Matt Diaz

10 Matt Diaz had (10) straight hits during three games in August 2006. He was 2 for 2 vs. Milwaukee on August 12, then he was 4 for 4 vs. Milwaukee on August 13, and he tied a league record on August 14, when he hit safely in his first four at bats vs. Washington. Diaz had seven singles, two doubles, a home run, and five RBIs.

John Smoltz

14 John Smoltz set an Atlanta record by winning (14) consecutive starts during his 1996 Cy Young season. Smoltzie lost his first start of the season, but then ran off 14 consecutive victories—and there were no bailouts in the bunch, he never had an off night, left early, had the team rally and get him off the hook kind of night, un-uh. He started and *won* 14 consecutive games.

John Smoltz

15 Smoltzie became the first Atlanta pitcher to record (15) strikeouts in a game when he mowed down the Expos on May 24, 1992. And 13 years later, he did it again. The second time was on April 10, 2005, vs. the New York Mets.

Chris Chambliss

20 Chris Chambliss set an Atlanta record with (20) pinch-hits in 1986. The veteran batted .311 in his final big league season, and he did a tremendous job off the bench. Chambliss batted .294 as a pinch-hitter. He was 20 for 68 with five doubles, one home run, nine RBIs, and nine walks.

Dan Uggla

33 Dan Uggla set an Atlanta record when he hit safely in (33) consecutive games in 2011. Tommy Holmes hit safely in 37 games for the 1945 Boston Braves, but Uggla's streak surpassed Rico Carty's 31-game streak in 1970 as the longest in Atlanta Braves history. The Braves' second baseman had been struggling, batting just .173 when the streak began on July 5. His average was at .231 when the streak ended. Manager Fredi Gonzalez said, "It was a streak where at any given time Chipper wasn't in the lineup and McCann wasn't in the lineup, and Uggla carried us. That was impressive." How impressive? Well, in those 33 games, Uggla also had 15 home runs and 32 RBIs.

Marcus Giles

49 Marcus Giles set an Atlanta record with (49) doubles in 2003. He nearly did it again, legging out 45 doubles in 2005. In both seasons, his total was the second highest in the league—but they also represent two of the top five season totals in franchise history. The other three: Hugh Duffy hit 51 doubles for the Beaneaters during his extraordinary 1894 season, Tommy Holmes hit 47 doubles for Boston in 1945, and Hank Aaron hit 46 doubles for Milwaukee in 1959.

Andruw Jones

51 Andruw Jones hit a franchise record (51) home runs in 2005. Jones hit only three during the season's first month, but he hit 13 in June and arrived at the All-Star break with 27. He had another big month in August, hitting 11 home runs with 29 RBIs. No surprise, Jones was the NL Player of the Month twice in 2005—in June, and again in August. Jones was second in league MVP balloting, but he was an All-Star and the home run champion, and he won another Gold Glove and his first Silver Slugger Award.

Gary Sheffield

52 Gary Sheffield set an Atlanta record when he reached base safely via a hit or a walk in (52) consecutive games in 2002. He hit .307 with a .404 on-base percentage for the season, but it was July and August when Sheffield caught fire. In July he batted .344 with 33 hits in 26 games, ten doubles, five home runs, 22 RBIs, and 12 walks—and then in August he batted .353 with 30 hits in 23 games, four doubles, six home runs, 15 RBIs, and 18 walks. Starting on May 31 and continuing for 52 games through July 27, Sheffield reached base safely in every game. Twice in that streak he failed to get a hit or walk, but both times his streak continued via a hit by pitch.

Chipper Jones

87 Chipper Jones set an Atlanta record with (87) extra-base hits during his 1999 MVP season. He also set franchise records by reaching base 309 times, amassing 359 total bases, and launching 45 home runs as a switch-hitter. Only one player in franchise history had a season with more extra-base hits: Hank Aaron had 92 for the Milwaukee Braves in 1959.

Dale Murphy

131 Dale Murphy set an Atlanta record when he scored (131) runs in 1983. Hugh Duffy scored 160 runs for the Beaneaters back in 1894, but prior to Murphy the highest total in the modern era was Hank Aaron's 127 in 1962. Rafael Furcal nearly eclipsed this record in 2003, scoring 130 runs as the Braves' offense set all sorts of team records.

Gary Sheffield

132 In his second season with the Braves, Gary Sheffield was an integral part of the most prolific offense in Atlanta history. The club established numerous records, and Sheffield got one of his own. Sheffield batted .330 with 39 home runs and (132) RBIs in 2003. No Atlanta player had previously come close to that number. If you go back to Hugh Duffy and the Beaneaters, he had 145 RBIs in 1894. In Milwaukee, Eddie Mathews had 135 and Hank Aaron had 132.

Greg Maddux

156 Greg Maddux set an Atlanta record with his (1.56) earned run average during his 1994 Cy Young season. He bested the 1.87 ERA that Phil Niekro put in the record book back in 1967. And in this category, there's no one from any other era of Braves history who even comes close to what Maddux did in 1994. In fact, the only person who did come close to what Maddux did in 1994 was ... Maddux in 1995, when he posted a 1.63 ERA—the second lowest in franchise history.

Ralph Garr

219 Ralph Garr set an Atlanta record with (219) hits in 1971. Felipe Alou set the standard in 1966, the Braves first season in Atlanta, with 218—and since then, Garr is the only player to eclipse Alou's total. There have been five 200-hit seasons in Atlanta, but only three players have achieved this feat: Garr and Alou both did it twice. Marquis Grissom is the only other player with a 200-hit season in Atlanta, though Andruw Jones (199), Terry Pendleton (199), and Rafael Furcal (194) all came close. Hugh Duffy (237) holds the premodern era record, Tommy Holmes (224) holds the record for the Boston era, and Hank Aaron (223) holds the record for the Milwaukee era in franchise history.

John Smoltz

276 John Smoltz led the league and set an Atlanta record with (276) strikeouts during his 1996 Cy Young season. It was a career high and the second strikeout title for Smoltz, who had a shot at winning the Triple Crown until his earned run average suffered towards the season's end. He led the league in wins and strikeouts, but was fourth in ERA. The previous Atlanta record was Phil Niekro's 262 in 1977. No other modern era player even comes close.

Rico Carty

366 Rico Carty led the league with a (.366) batting average and .454 on-base percentage in 1970. Both numbers established Atlanta records as well. Rogers Hornsby has the highest modern era average in franchise history, batting .387 in 1928. Chipper Jones made a run at these same two records in 2008—he batted .364, falling just short of the batting record, but his .470 on-base percentage allowed him to move ahead of Carty in the record book at least once.

Hank Aaron

669 There's a bit of controversy over this one. Hank Aaron slugged (.669) and established a career high with 47 home runs in 1971. His home run total would stand as the Atlanta record until Andruw Jones in 2005, but his slugging percentage also established an Atlanta record that still stands ... sort of. Javy Lopez slugged .687 in his monstrous 2003 season when he hit 43 home runs in only 457 at bats. So you see the problem? Lopez did in fact post a higher slugging percentage than Aaron, but for official purposes such as establishing team records, well ... he needed more plate appearances to qualify. Could make for a tricky trivia question, I suppose ...

Greg Maddux

905 We touched on this one previously but it's worth mentioning again. Greg Maddux's (.905) winning percentage in 1995 was not only ridiculous, it also set an Atlanta record that will likely never be broken. Remember, Mad Dog was 13-0 on the road that season. He was 8-1 before the All-Star break, and 11-1 after the break.

"He ought to will his body to medical science."
— Hall of Famer Carl Hubbell, after watching 42-year-old Warren Spahn pitch 16 innings and throw 201 pitches vs. San Francisco

10 FABULOUS FEATS

HOME RUN BARRAGES, epic pitching duels, rare hitting feats, unexpected debuts, and monstrous seasons ... all that and more are on tap here in the final chapter.

What did little known Albert Hall do that Hank Aaron never achieved his entire career? What did Adam LaRoche do in his first big league game that no rookie in National League history had ever done before? What did Chipper Jones do in 1999 that no player in *Major League history* had ever done before? And what did Andres Galarraga, Andruw Jones, Chipper Jones, and Javy Lopez achieve as teammates in 1998 that no other teammates in franchise history had achieved?

Read on ... its all here, as we look at 25 of the greatest feats in franchise history, by the numbers.

Jason Heyward

1 It took Jason Heyward exactly (1) swing to kick start his Major

League career. The first swing of his career was a three-run bomb. Chipper Jones called the ovation following Heyward's 2010 Opening Day home run the loudest he'd ever heard.

Adam LaRoche

2 Adam LaRoche made his big league debut on April 7, 2004. In that game he did something that no player in NL history had ever done in his first Major League game—he got (2) hits in the same inning. Trailing the Mets 6-3 in the home half of the fourth, LaRoche singled, doubled, scored twice, and drove in two runs as the Braves erupted for 11 runs en route to an 18-10 victory.

Back-to-Back-to-Back

3 Atlanta hit (3) consecutive home runs vs. Cincinnati on May 28, 2003. A rarity, but it does happen. What made the Braves' slugfest extraordinary was *when* it occurred … the first three batters of the game. It was just the second time in Major League history that a team hit three consecutive home runs to start a game. Rafael Furcal led off the game, followed by Mark DeRosa and Gary Sheffield. Javy Lopez added another home run later in the same inning and the Braves rolled to a 15-3 win.

40 Home Runs

3 The Braves offense produced (3) 40-homer guys in 1973,

establishing a Major League record: Hank Aaron (40), Darrell Evans (41), and Davey Johnson (43).

30 Home Runs

4 The Braves offense produced (4) 30-homer guys in 1998 for the first time in franchise history, tying a Major League record shared by several teams: Andres Galarraga (44), Andruw Jones (31), Chipper Jones (34), and Javy Lopez (34).

Albert Hall

5 Albert Hall hit (5) career home runs for the Braves. The speedster batted only 805 times over parts of eight seasons. Hall set career highs with 33 steals and three home runs in 1987 when he got the bulk of his playing time. And on September 23, 1987, on the same day he hit his third career home run, Hall also had a single, double, and triple to become the first player in Atlanta history to hit for the cycle. A cycle is an exceptionally rare feat, all the more so for a guy who hit only five bombs his whole career. After all, Hank Aaron hit 755 home runs, 98 triples, and 624 doubles among his 3,771 career hits ... and he never hit for the cycle. Albert Hall had only five homers, eight triples, 37 doubles, and 202 career hits. Three players hit for the cycle during the Boston era in franchise history: Duff Cooley, John Bates, and William Collins. On August 14, 2008, Mark Kotsay became the second Atlanta player to hit for the cycle.

Brian McCann

5 Brian McCann won his (5th) Silver Slugger Award in 2011. He's the first player in franchise history to win the award five times, and he's won it four years in a row. McCann is just the sixth catcher in Major League history to win the Silver Slugger as many as five times: Mike Piazza, Ivan Rodriguez, Lance Parrish, Gary Carter, and Jorge Posada are the others.

Deion Sanders

6 Deion Sanders scored (6) points on September 10, 1989. Not runs, *points*. Okay, he didn't score for the Braves—it was for the Atlanta Falcons. The 21-year-old rookie scored a touchdown in his first career NFL game. Sanders, who later played for the Braves from 1991-94, was also a rookie for the New York Yankees in September 1989. And that touchdown made him the first player in history to hit a Major League home run and score an NFL touchdown *in the same week*.

Ryan Klesko

8 Atlanta hit (8) home runs vs. Cleveland during the 1995 World Series. Fred McGriff had a big home run in Game 1, and of course David Justice had the biggest in Game 6 ... but also in that series, not only did Ryan Klesko hit three of the Braves' eight home runs, he hit them all on the road. It was the first time in Major League history that a player homered in three consecutive road games in a single World Series.

Warren Spahn

17 Hall of Fame pitcher Warren Spahn could make even the best hitters look pretty ridiculous at the plate. Ironically, Spahn was also one of the game's best hitting pitchers. He belted at least one home run in (17) consecutive seasons and homered an NL record 35 times during his career—two short of the Major League record for pitchers.

Greg Maddux

18 Greg Maddux set a Major League record when he won (18) consecutive road decisions from 1994-95. It's honestly hard to say which is more extraordinary ... the fact he won 18 consecutive decisions, or that he posted a miniscule 0.99 earned run average during his streak.

Greg Maddux

20 This might be the best illustration of just how dominant Greg Maddux was during his prime. In 1997, Maddux pitched 232 innings and walked only (20) batters. He won 19 games ... *and walked only 20 batters.* No one in history has ever had a ratio of wins-to-walks that approaches what Maddux did that year. The success Braves' pitchers had in the 1990s is hard to overstate. That same year, in August 1997, Maddux and his teammates Tom Glavine, John Smoltz, and Denny Neagle combined to make 19 consecutive starts in which *none of them* gave up more than three earned runs in any given game.

1998

25 The Braves set a NL record by homering in (25) consecutive games in 1998. Ryan Klesko hit a two-run homer during a 10-2 victory vs. St. Louis on May 13 to set the record for Atlanta. The 1941 Yankees and the 1994 Tigers are the only other teams to homer in 25 consecutive games. The Braves hit 43 total homers during the streak.

Fred McGriff

30 Fred McGriff led the Braves with a .318 average, 34 home runs, and 94 RBIs in 1994 ... and keep in mind that season was cut short due to the strike. McGriff only played 113 games. And despite that, he became just the ninth player in Major League history to post seven consecutive seasons with (30) or more home runs.

Team No-No

81 Atlanta's pitching staff gave up just (8.1) hits per nine innings in 1991. The staff had the third best earned run average in the league, but no team gave up fewer hits. And on September 11, 1991, the staff didn't give up *any* hits at all during a 1-0 victory vs. San Diego. It was the first combined no-hitter in National League history. Kent Mercker got the win, tossing six innings and giving up just two walks. Mark Wohlers pitched two innings of perfect relief. And Alejandro Pena pitched a perfect ninth for the save. It was the first no-hitter for the Braves since Phil Niekro tossed one on August 5, 1973. Three years later, Kent Mercker would pitch a complete game no-hitter vs. Los Angeles, making him just the second pitcher in franchise history (after Warren Spahn) to take part in two no-hitters for the Braves.

Andruw Jones

100 Andruw Jones hit 368 home runs for the Braves but it's often overlooked how powerful he was at such a young age. He was the fifth youngest player in Major League history to reach (100) career home runs. He was a 19-year-old rookie when he made his big league debut on August 15, 1996, and he was only 23-years and two-months old on June 24, 2000, when he took Milwaukee's Jamey Wright out of the park for his 100th career blast.

Warren Spahn

201 About 16,000 fans were on hand at Candlestick Park on July 2, 1963, to witness one of the most memorable pitching duels in baseball history. A 42-year-old Warren Spahn threw (201) pitches during a 16-inning marathon vs. the Giants—and a 25-year-old Juan Marichal threw 227 pitches for the Giants. Alvin Dark, the Giants manager, visited Marichal on the mound in the ninth, tenth, eleventh, thirteenth, and fourteenth innings, when finally Marichal reportedly said to him, "Do you see that man pitching for the other side? Do you know that man is 42-years-old? I'm only 25. If that man is on the mound, nobody is going to take me out of here." And no one did. Spahn and Marichal both pitched complete games, but the Giants prevailed when Willie Mays homered against Spahn with one out in the bottom of the sixteenth inning.

Chipper Jones

319 The batting average (.319) for Chipper Jones during his 1999 MVP season. Statistically, he had one of the best seasons in baseball history and became the first player ever to achieve all of the following in the same year: .300-plus average, .400-plus on-base percentage (.441), .600-plus slugging percentage (.633), 40-plus home runs (45), 40-plus doubles (41), 100-plus walks (126), 100-plus RBIs (110), 100-plus runs (116), 20-plus steals (25).

Otis Nixon

333 Otis Nixon recorded (333) putouts playing outfield during 120 games for the Braves in 1992. One catch in particular stands out. Most players never make a play as spectacular or as important as the one Nixon made that season—even guys who play a decade or longer. Atlanta's 13-game winning streak in July 1992 catapulted the club into first place, and that streak was capped off with a 1-0 victory vs. Pittsburgh on July 25. The Braves offense managed only one hit that day, but it was a solo home run by David Justice. Charlie Leibrandt, Alejandro Pena, and Kent Mercker combined on a five-hitter for Atlanta—but it took a spectacular ninth-inning catch by Nixon to preserve the shutout. "I was in a daze. That's the best play I ever saw," said David Justice, after Nixon robbed the Pirates' Andy Van Slyke of a two-run homer. The *New York Times* described it this way: "[He] was in full stride when he leaped on the padded ten-foot fence and reached over it for the game-saving catch."

Sid Bream

351 Sid Bream scored (351) runs during his Major League career. He also scored nine runs in the postseason—including the most important run of his life, and one of the most memorable in Major League postseason history. Bream scored the Pennant-winning run vs. Pittsburgh in the 1992 National League Championship Series. He scored from second base on Francisco Cabrera's clutch two-out hit, and if it's possible to categorize something as a "slow dash" then

Breams' heroic effort, though agonizingly painful to watch, certainly qualifies. Jimy Williams waved him home though, and Bream gave every ounce of efficiency and energy that his battle-worn body had to offer—and then some.

Warren Spahn

356 Warren Spahn won 363 career games—the most in Major League history by a left handed pitcher, and the sixth most in history overall. Spahn won (356) of those games for the Braves.

Chipper Jones

400 Chipper Jones batted (.400) vs. the New York Mets during his 1999 MVP campaign. Chipper was 16 for 40 during 12 games vs. the Mets with a 1.000 slugging percentage—he hit three doubles and seven home runs with 16 RBIs. He officially became known as a "Met Killer" when he homered four times, scored five runs, and picked up seven RBIs during a crucial three-game sweep vs. New York in late September. The Mets entered the series trailing by just two games and were looking to end the Braves' run of Division Titles. No such luck.

No-No

506 Warren Spahn faced just 29 batters and pitched a no-hitter vs. Philadelphia in a 4-0 victory on September 16, 1960. It was his 20th win of the season and the 11th time he'd reached that milestone—

but after (506) career Major League starts, it was his first no-hitter. Only a month earlier his teammate, Lew Burdette, had also pitched a no-hitter vs. Philadelphia. It was the first—and so far only—time in franchise history that the Braves recorded two no-hitters in the same season. As for Spahn, it took him a long time to notch his first no-no, but it took him only six more starts before he got number two. On April 28, 1961, in career start number 512, he no-hit the Giants, facing the minimum 27 batters in a 1-0 victory and becoming the first player in franchise history to pitch a pair of no-hitters.

Gene Conley

782 The earned run average (7.82) for Gene Conley in 1952. He was 0-3 as a 21-year-old rookie for the Boston Braves. Hardly remarkable, right? Well, Conley's story was just beginning. Two years later he was an All-Star who won 14 games for the Milwaukee Braves. And how did the 6' 8" pitcher spend his time between stints in the big leagues? Playing for the Boston Celtics, of course. After his breakthrough 1954 season, however, he stayed with the Braves and eventually won the World Series with the 1957 club. Well, that wasn't enough, either. Conley went back to the Celtics and won three NBA World Championships ... while he was still pitching for the Braves, Phillies, and Red Sox. Conley is the only professional athlete to win both a World Series title and a World Championship in another major sport. Additionally, he's the only professional athlete to play for three different franchises in one city: the Boston Braves, Boston Celtics, and Boston Red Sox.

Hank Aaron

762* Barry Bonds hit a Major League record (762*) home runs. He was a great ballplayer and it was fun to watch him play when the Pirates or Giants came to town. It was especially fun watching him bat .148 vs. the Braves during the 1991 League Championship Series … it was decidedly less fun watching him hit three home runs vs. the Braves in the 2002 Division Series. Hank Aaron hit 755 career home runs—733 for the Braves and 22 for the Brewers. All things considered (Aaron never cheated), it seems appropriate for Braves' fans to continue referring to Aaron as Baseball's All-Time Home Run Champion.

ABOUT THE AUTHOR

TUCKER ELLIOT IS a Georgia native and a diehard Braves fan. A former high school athletic director and varsity baseball coach, he now resides and writes fulltime in Tampa, FL.

REFERENCES

WEBSITES
Baseball-reference.com
MLB.com (and the official team sites through MLB.com)
BaseballHallofFame.org
ESPN.com

BOOKS
Baseball, an Illustrated History, Geoffrey C. Ward and Ken Burns
The Team by Team Encyclopedia of Major League Baseball, Dennis Purdy
The Unofficial Guide to Baseball's Most Unusual Records, Bob Mackin
The 2005 ESPN Baseball Encyclopedia, edited by Pete Palmer and Gary
        Gillette
100 Years of the World Series, Eric Enders

ABOUT BLACK MESA

Look for these titles in the popular Trivia IQ Series:

- *Atlanta Braves*
- *New York Yankees*
- *Cincinnati Reds*
- *Boston Red Sox (Volumes (I & II)*
- *Milwaukee Brewers*
- *St. Louis Cardinals (Volumes I & II)*
- *Major League Baseball*
- *Mixed Martial Arts (Volumes I & II)*
- *Boston Celtics (Volumes I & II)*
- *University of Florida Gators Football*
- *University of Georgia Bulldogs Football*
- *University of Oklahoma Sooners Football*
- *University of Texas Longhorns Football*
- *Texas A&M Aggies Football*
- *West Point Football*
- *New England Patriots*
- *Buffalo Bills*

For information about special discounts for bulk purchases, please email:

black.mesa.publishing@gmail.com

www.blackmesabooks.com

The following is an excerpt from

Major League Baseball IQ: The Ultimate Test of True Fandom

TUCKER ELLIOT

Available from Black Mesa Publishing

"It isn't that hard to get RBIs when you're hitting home runs—you generally get at least one."
— Mike Schmidt

FIRST

THERE'S A REASON diehard fans get to the ballpark hours before game time. It's not for better parking. It's not for extra time to find our seats. It's not so we'll have time to down an extra hot dog, heavy on the mustard, prior to the first pitch.

It's called BP.

Watching a Major League team take batting practice is without question one of the most exhilarating events a baseball fan can witness firsthand. But we don't go hours early to watch players practice hitting to the opposite field. Oh no, we want to see the long ball, and lots of them. That's why we bring our gloves. It's partly because we want to chase those big flies and try to catch one like we're little kids ... and partly because we know if Albert Pujols drills one right at us that having a glove is truly a matter of life or death.

There isn't a fan alive that doesn't love the long ball.

So that's where we begin. Here in the top of the first we've got a heavy dose of big-time sluggers who performed some incredible feats. Let's get going with those two immortal words we love so much: *Play Ball!*

TOP OF THE FIRST

QUESTION 1: The annual Home Run Derby during the All-Star break has been a fan-favorite for a long time. The All-Star break has also been a historical measuring stick for players on a potential record-setting home run pace. If you've got 30 bombs at the break, well, that's pretty special. Who was the first player in history to hit 30 home runs before the All-Star break?
- a) Dave Kingman
- b) Willie Mays
- c) Harmon Killebrew
- d) Mike Schmidt

QUESTION 2: The list of players to hit 30 homers before the break is pretty short, but it's also pretty stout because it's a virtual who's who of home run champions. A few guys have done it more than once, but only one player has made it to the break with 30 homers on four different occasions. Who is that player?
- a) Ken Griffey, Jr.
- b) Sammy Sosa
- c) Mark McGwire
- d) Alex Rodriguez

QUESTION 3: In 1994, for the first time in history, there were three players who hit 30 homers prior to the All-Star break. In 1998, that record was eclipsed as four players went into the break with at least 30 homers. In both seasons—1994 and 1998—there was one slugger who was a part of both of those record-setting groups. Who had at least 30 homers at the All-Star break in both 1994 and 1998?
- a) Greg Vaughn
- b) Mark McGwire
- c) Ken Griffey, Jr.
- d) Sammy Sosa

QUESTION 4: Who is the only slugger in history to make it to the All-Star break with at least 30 homers ... for two different teams?
- a) Ken Griffey, Jr.
- b) Mark McGwire

    c)   Reggie Jackson
    d)   Greg Vaughn

QUESTION 5: Only five players in history have made it to the All-Star break with at least 35 home runs. The record is 39. Who holds that record?
    a)   Mark McGwire
    b)   Luis Gonzalez
    c)   Ken Griffey, Jr.
    d)   Barry Bonds

QUESTION 6: Who was the first player in history to make it to the All-Star break with at least 30 homers and *not* win his league's home run title?
    a)   Reggie Jackson
    b)   Greg Vaughn
    c)   Willie Mays
    d)   Dave Kingman

QUESTION 7: Frank Thomas—not the Big Hurt, but the original Frank Thomas who debuted for the Pittsburgh Pirates on August 17, 1951, and finished his initial rookie campaign with two home runs—slugged 30 homers in 1953, his first full big league season, and was an All-Star the following year. He later set a Major League record for a particular type of home run—that being the clutch walk-off game-winning variety. Thomas was the first player in big league history to win a game for each of four different franchises via a walk-off home run: the Pirates, Braves, Mets, and Phillies. Over the years several other players have tied his record, most recently a high-profile free agent signee in his first year with his new club in 2010. His game-winning shot came vs. Scot Shields of the LA Angels. Who tied the Major League record by hitting a walk-off blast for his fourth ballclub on May 1, 2010?
    a)   Johnny Damon
    b)   Alfonso Soriano
    c)   Andruw Jones
    d)   Troy Glaus

QUESTION 8: And staying with that particular home run record ... prior to 2010, it was a member of the Tampa Bay Rays who tied this record by drilling a walk-off blast for his fourth different team. Who tied this record as a member of the Rays?
a)   Vinny Castilla
b)   Jose Canseco
c)   Carlos Pena
d)   Fred McGriff

QUESTION 9: On May 1, 2010, a member of the Arizona Diamondbacks doubled and singled in his first two at bats vs. the Cubs to raise his season average to .667. Okay, he was only 9 for 12 on the season ... but, he did start the season *9 for 12*, and even better the player who got off to such a hot start at the plate in 2010 was Dan Haren, who doesn't earn the big paycheck to swing the bat, but rather to make other guys who also earn big paychecks look flat-out stupid trying to make contact with Uncle Charlie. In nearly 40 years of baseball since the DH rule was instituted in the AL only one other pitcher had a better stretch of at bats than Haren's run to begin 2010. A member of the 2001 San Francisco Giants pitching staff had a stretch in which he was 12 for 13. Now that's just ridiculous. Which member of the 2001 Giants pitching staff apparently thought he was Barry Bonds for a spell?
a)   Jason Schmidt
b)   Kirk Rueter
c)   Russ Ortiz
d)   Livan Hernandez

QUESTION 10: The Los Angeles Dodgers are steeped in history and tradition, recognized around the world as one of the premiere franchises in professional sports, not just MLB. So to have your name etched in the Dodgers' franchise record book for something no one else has ever done is quite special to say the least. This is the franchise, after all, of Reese, Lasorda, Snider, Koufax, Campanella, Robinson, Drysdale, and ... Don Demeter? Yup, Demeter, who hit only 34 home runs in five seasons for the Dodgers, set a franchise record in 1959 that stood half a century. It was a hot start at the plate that got Demeter's name in the book after he belted five homers with 14 RBI and a .382 batting average during the first nine home games on the Dodgers' schedule that season. No other Dodgers' player had ever posted such gaudy numbers in the three Triple Crown categories during the club's first nine home games ... and no player did so again, not until 2010 that is, when this player batted *.432* with five home runs and 14 RBI during the Dodgers first nine home games. Who set the new standard for hot starts at home for the Dodgers franchise?

a) Matt Kemp
b) Manny Ramirez
c) Andre Ethier
d) James Loney

TOP OF THE FIRST ANSWER KEY

___ **QUESTION 1:** B
___ **QUESTION 2:** C
___ **QUESTION 3:** C
___ **QUESTION 4:** B
___ **QUESTION 5:** D
___ **QUESTION 6:** C
___ **QUESTION 7:** A*
___ **QUESTION 8:** C*
___ **QUESTION 9:** D*
___ **QUESTION 10:** C

KEEP A RUNNING TALLY OF YOUR CORRECT ANSWERS!

Number correct: ___ / 10

Overall correct: ___ / 10

#7 – Royals, Red Sox, Yankees, and Tigers.
#8 – Athletics, Tigers, Red Sox, and Rays.
#9 – He was 15 for 64 on the season: .296, one home run, eight RBI, and only four strikeouts.

BOTTOM OF THE FIRST

QUESTION 11: The National League began play in 1876, thus the player who led the league in home runs that season was, for a brief time, baseball's all-time leading home run hitter. His name was George Hall and he played in Philadelphia. And as the baseball gods often orchestrate, the stars were aligned just so and the result is this obscure yet fascinating bit of trivia: on July 15, 1876, when Hall homered for the final time that season (therefore, setting the first-ever season home run record) on that same day George Bradley, pitching for St. Louis, tossed the first-ever no-hitter in big league history. Bradley won 45 games that season and enjoyed a much longer and more successful career than did Hall, who the following season was homerless and later banned from baseball for fixing games. Still, he was baseball's first home run champ. How many home runs did it take for George Hall to establish the first season home run record in 1876?

a) 3
b) 5
c) 7
d) 9

QUESTION 12: George Hall's home run record lasted three years. Boston's Charley Jones broke it in 1879, and unlike Hall, Jones continued to produce and enjoy big league success, setting another record the following season when he became the first player in history to hit two home runs in the same inning. How many home runs did Charley Jones hit in 1879 to establish a new big league record?

a) 5
b) 7
c) 9
d) 11

QUESTION 13: Harry Stovey tied for the league lead with six home runs in 1880, and then in 1883 the five-time home run champion broke the season record previously set by Charley Jones when he hit 14 four-baggers. That same season, Cincinnati, in the American Association, established a professional record by belting 35 home runs ... as a team! Well, both the individual and team records didn't last long. That's because in 1884 Chicago and Ned Williamson went on a power binge. Williamson shattered the home run record with *27* (and became the first player to hit three homers in a single game) and his club belted *142 long balls*. The top four home run hitters in the league all played for Chicago! And the reason for this power surge was ...

    a)   Rampant HGH usage

    b)   Corked bats

    c)   Greg Anderson's (Barry Bonds' trainer) great-great-great-grandfather was Chicago's trainer that year

    d)   Lakefront Park dimensions (where Chicago played its home games): 196 feet to right, 252 to right-center, 300 to left-center, and 180 down the left field line

QUESTION 14: Ned Williamson's home run record stood for 35 years. Babe Ruth, who led the league with 11 home runs in 1918, blasted 29 home runs in 1919 to establish a new record. The record-breaking blast came in the ninth with his team trailing 1-0. It tied the score, sent the game to extra-innings, and Ruth's club won it in the thirteenth inning. Against which team did Babe Ruth break the single-season home run record for the first time in his career?

    a)   Boston Red Sox

    b)   New York Yankees

    c)   Detroit Tigers

    d)   St. Louis Browns

QUESTION 15: The year Ruth hit 60 home runs, in 1927, he and Lou Gehrig established a Major League record for teammates, combining for 107 home runs. That record fell on September 9, 1961, when Roger Maris homered vs. Cleveland for his 56th long ball of the season—and combined with the 52 Mickey Mantle had at the time, gave the powerful duo 108 on the season. Maris, of course, went on to break Ruth's single-season record when he went yard on October 1—the season's final day—for his 61st home run. Against which team did Maris homer to break Ruth's single-season home run record?

    a)   Boston Red Sox

    b)   Detroit Tigers

c) Chicago White Sox
d) Cleveland Indians

QUESTION 16: A big home run is a definite game-changer—and a pinch-hit home run, well, that's really special. What about a guy who consistently belts pinch-hit home runs? You get a guy like that on your team and good things are bound to happen. Only one player in Major League history has hit as many as four pinch-hit home runs in back-to-back seasons. Who is he?

a) George Crowe
b) Gates Brown
c) Cliff Johnson
d) Lenny Harris

QUESTION 17: How about the Major League record for most pinch-hit home runs in one season? Joe Cronin holds the A.L. record with five for the 1943 Boston Red Sox, but he was one short of the then Major League record six set by Brooklyn's Johnny Frederick in 1932. Frederick's record stood until 2000. A member of the Dodgers hit seven pinch-hit home runs in 2000 to establish a new record, and the following season, a member of the Pittsburgh Pirates tied the new record when he also hit seven pinch-hit home runs. Can you identify the two players with seven pinch-hit homers in 2000 and 2001?

a) Devon White and Gary Matthews
b) Todd Hollandsworth and Brian Giles
c) Dave Hansen and Craig Wilson
d) Jim Leyritz and John Vander Wal

QUESTION 18: Staying with the pinch-hitters … Lenny Harris pinch-hit a N.L. record 804 times during his career and his 212 hits in that role is also a record. The leader in the A.L. is Gates Brown, who pinch-hit 414 times. The big difference? All of Brown's pinch-hit appearances came for the Detroit Tigers, but Harris … he was a journeyman. For how many different N.L. teams did Lenny Harris get at least one pinch-hit?

a) 6
b) 7

    c)   8
    d)   9

QUESTION 19: The Major League record for hitting safely in consecutive pinch-hit at bats during one season is eight. Dave Philley established this record with Philadelphia in 1958. That record has never been broken, although it has been equaled. Who besides Dave Philley is the only other player in baseball history to collect eight consecutive pinch-hits?
    a)   Lenny Harris
    b)   Rusty Staub
    c)   Randy Bush
    d)   John Vander Wal

QUESTION 20: Gates Brown owns the A.L. record with 16 career pinch-hit homers. Jerry Lynch (Cincinnati and Pittsburgh) holds the N.L. record with 18 pinch-hit homers. The player who owns the Major League record isn't all that close to being the leader in either league, because he obviously spent time playing in both the N.L. and the A.L. Who hit a Major League record 20 pinch-hit home runs during his career?
    a)   Rich Reese
    b)   Ron Northey
    c)   Cliff Johnson
    d)   Rusty Staub

Bottom of the First Answer Key

___ **Question 11:** B
___ **Question 12:** C
___ **Question 13:** D*
___ **Question 14:** B
___ **Question 15:** A
___ **Question 16:** A
___ **Question 17:** C
___ **Question 18:** C
___ **Question 19:** B
___ **Question 20:** C

Keep a running tally of your correct answers!

Number correct: ___ / 10

Overall correct: ___ / 20

#13 – Prior to 1884, ground rules mandated balls hit over the left and right field fences were deemed doubles, but in 1884 they were ruled home runs.